Religious diversity and intercultural education: a reference book for schools

John Keast
Editor

Council of Europe Publishing
F-67075 Strasbourg Cedex
http://book.coe.int

ISBN 978-92-871-6223-6
© Council of Europe, March 2007
Reprinted September 2007, October 2008
Printed at the Council of Europe

Acknowledgments

This publication has benefited enormously from the contributions provided by the experts designated to develop this part of the Council of Europe project entitled "The new challenge of intercultural education: religious diversity and dialogue in Europe" (2002-2005): César Bîrzea (Romania), Robert Jackson (United Kingdom), John Keast (United Kingdom), Heid Leganger-Krogstad (Norway), Micheline Milot (Canada), Albert Raasch (Germany), Micheline Rey (Switzerland), Peter Schreiner (Germany), as well as from the assistance of Villano Qiriazi of the Council of Europe Directorate of Education.

Special thanks should also be addressed to the Ministry of Education of Norway for the strong financial support given to this project and to the members of the Steering Committee for Education of the Council of Europe from Austria, Cyprus, France, Germany, Greece, the Holy See, Norway, Slovenia, Spain and the United Kingdom, for selecting in their countries the examples of current practice presented in this book and for their written contributions: Gabriele Hösch-Schagar (Austria), Andreas Skotinos (Cyprus), Tim Jensen (Denmark), Sylvie Aymard (France), Vassiliki Makri and the Jewish Museum of Greece, Daniela Rossi (Italy), Margareth H. Danson (Norway), Gorahnka Kreacic (Slovenia), Julia Ipgrave (United Kingdom), Kevin O'Grady (United Kingdom), Amy Whittall (United Kingdom), Naina Parma (United Kingdom), Lat Blaylock (United Kingdom).

Our warmest thanks go in particular to Pieter Batelaan (Netherlands), former president of the International Association for Intercultural Education, who was one of the initiators of this project.

Contents

Part II. Educational conditions and methodological approaches
Introduction
A. Educational conditions
Chapter 1 – Co-operative learning

Chapter 2 – A "safe space" to foster self-expression

Chapter 3 – Use of "distancing" and "simulation"

Chapter 4 – Empathetic communication

B. Learning approaches
Chapter 1 – The phenomenological approach

Part IV. Examples of current practice

Part V. References

Introduction:

Intercultural Learning

1. The education policy perspective

Cesar Bîrzéa

This reference book is the main outcome of the project entitled "The challenge of intercultural education today: religious diversity and dialogue in Europe", developed by the Council of Europe between 2002 and 2005. This project was established by the Council following the events of 9/11. The then Secretary General, Walter Schwimmer, had the foresight to see that those events would bring the religious dimension to the fore in politics, education and society all over the world. There would be a real need to improve the effectiveness of intercultural education across Europe if people and societies were not to become even more divided.

The project develops a new dimension on intercultural education in Europe by addressing the religious diversity inherent to our multicultural societies, schools included, from the human rights and intercultural learning perspective. Its purpose is not so much to examine religious education and the role it plays in official curricula but to construct an approach to intercultural learning that promotes dialogue, mutual understanding and living together. Such an approach differs from the monoreligious and monocultural approach still to be found in many European curricula. Indeed, it could be argued not that we have too much religious education but that we have too little or none at all. Our major concern is that we tend to ignore or marginalise some important values in giving priority to knowledge and short-term results, instead of focusing on what education is really for and on individual and social development.

Religious and moral values are a highly sensitive area, involving beliefs and concepts about the world. Such values cannot be approached simply from a narrow curricular perspective, nor can they be reduced to a mere transmission of knowledge. They must be developed gradually, with pupils becoming aware of and acquiring such values individually and to lasting effect. In other words, acquisition of religious and moral values must be the outcome of real individual experience and skill. Similarly, the development of religious and moral convictions must be consistent with democratic values as a whole, namely respect for human rights, pluralism and the rule of law. Given this perspective, the learning approaches, methods and experiences presented in this reference book are based on three principles:

- religion is an important cultural fact (similar to other identity sources such as languages, history or cultural heritage);
- beliefs about the world and values must be developed gradually, based on real personal and social learning experiences;
- an integrated approach to spiritual, religious, moral and civic values must be encouraged.

Intercultural education is addressed at three levels:

- at the level of education policies, in the form of clear-cut educational aims and purposes;
- at the level of institutions, especially through democratic governance, student participation, open learning settings and inclusive policies;
- at teaching level, through the approaches and methods that make up the very substance of the reference book.

The first level is clearly supported by a series of political documents in favour of intercultural education recently adopted in the context of the Council of Europe. We refer to:

- The Final Declaration of the 21st session of the Standing Conference of European Ministers of Education (Athens, 10-12 November 2003), devoted particularly to intercultural education;[1]
- The Wroclaw Declaration (9-10 December 2004) on the new context of cultural cooperation in Europe;
- The Action Plan adopted by the Third Summit of Heads of States and Governments (Warsaw, 16-17 May 2005) which refers explicitly to inter-cultural dialogue and issues specific to religious diversity.

In the Athens Declaration, European Ministers of education "11. Request the Council ... to

  a. relaunch conceptual research on intercultural education

  b. Help build understanding ... by introducing respect for human rights and diversity ... inter-religious dialogue ...

  c. Step up efforts in the area of content of learning methods and teaching aids ...

---

1. http://www.coe.int/T/E/Cultural_Co-operation/education/Standing_conferences/ e.21stsessionathens2003.asp#TopOfPage

d. Develop analytical instruments and identify and disseminate examples of good practice ... in school text books ...

e. Develop programmes aimed at communication and mutual understanding, particularly through language learning ...

f. Encourage member states to introduce the intercultural dimension into their education policies ...

g. Encourage research focusing on social learning and co-operative learning ...

h. Support initiatives and experiments with democratic governance in schools ...

i. Develop quality assurance instruments inspired by education for democratic citizenship, taking account of the intercultural dimension ...

j. Identify models of good practice ...

k. Strengthen intercultural education and management of diversity in its training ...

l. Devise and promote methodologies that are suitable to integrate into states' own initial and in-service training ...

m. Recognise the potential of ICT as a tool ...

n. Develop educational strategies and working methods to prepare teachers to manage new situations ...

o. Encourage the development of professional competencies for the teaching profession ...

p. Foster a global approach to institutional life ... taking account of the hidden curriculum, school atmosphere, organisational ethos and non-formal education ...

q. Encourage member states to acknowledge that managing diversity is not a problem in schools alone, but concerns the whole of society ..."

The main purpose of this reference book is, then, to help put these European aspirations into practice. The reference book assists policy makers, teachers, trainers and other education practitioners to address issues of religious diversity based on respect for human rights. This requires the development of intercultural competence in the case of pupils from widely differing social, cultural and religious backgrounds. This generic competence presupposes, in turn, other specific competences:

- sensitivity to a variety of cultural and religious sources of human diversity;
- ability to communicate with others and enter into dialogue;
- skills for learning to live together such as teamwork, cooperative learning, empathic communication, peaceful conflict resolution, confidence building;
- capacity to explore beliefs, practices, symbols and rituals, and deal with any sensitive and controversial issues raised;
- critical thinking and individual reflection.

This reference book is the outcome of cooperation between various practitioners (teachers and other educational staff, teacher-trainers) and researchers. Its origins lie in an extensive survey on the intercultural approach to European diversity which brought together representatives of most member states. The link between research and practice is plain to see in the structure of the reference book, which moves from theory to practice.

2. How to use this reference book

John Keast

This reference book is intended to help teachers, teacher trainers, administrators, policy makers and others deal with the important issue of religious diversity in Europe's schools. The religious dimension of intercultural education is an issue that affects all schools, whether they are religiously diverse or not, because their pupils live and will work in increasingly diverse societies.

The introduction traces the development of the project at the Council of Europe that has resulted in the publication of this reference book. It also shows how it is securely located in the history, nature, values and priorities of the Council and other European initiatives.

The first main section of the reference book covers some of the theoretical perspectives that teachers and others need to be aware of as they consider issues of intercultural education. This section is rooted in the experience and expertise of educational and intercultural experts centrally involved in exploring and articulating these perspectives not just in Europe but across the world. Readers are asked to reflect on the importance of a sound theoretical underpinning for considering matters of educational practice.

The second section begins to relate the conceptual elements of intercultural education to various approaches to teaching and learning. Here a number of key educational considerations are taken into account, and some methodological approaches are described, based upon research and practice in several European contexts. Again, these have been developed over many years by a variety of experts in the field of teacher education, training and support. Each approach is illustrated with examples. It is important for readers to realise that the religious dimension of intercultural education and intercultural education itself require specific kinds of teaching and learning approaches. Unlike some traditional approaches to intercultural education, these methods focus not on the link between the dominant culture (for example dominant religion) and minority cultures (for example minority religions), but instead on learning to live together. The reference point is not the differences between several cultural communities but the manner of resolving common issues and working on joint projects.

The third section of the reference book deals with wider questions of religious diversity in schools in different settings; that is, it goes beyond the curriculum to school governance and management. It deals with how to apply intercultural education principles (participation, inclusion and respect for human rights) in different education settings: in public and faith schools, formal and non-formal learning, management and school governance. There is unanimity in the view that effective teaching and learning about religious diversity in the curriculum are not possible unless they are consistent with, and reinforced by, good practice on the wider front in education.

The fourth section of the reference book consists of some examples of current practice in some member states of the Council of Europe. As is to be expected, such practice is very variable. The examples show different levels of expertise; they are not all as good as each other, and are not offered as models to be slavishly followed. Rather these examples provide an opportunity for readers to reflect on their own and others' practice, and apply the insights offered in previous sections of the reference book to real classroom and other practice.

The reference book is designed to be user-friendly and structured so as to:

- stimulate the use of inspiring methods and practices in a wide range of contexts, especially at primary and secondary education level;

- prompt practitioners to realise how activities may be both inserted into school subjects (for example citizenship education, social studies, religious education), and developed by means of cross-curricular themes (for example local issues, religious manifestations, conflict management), and even included in certain extra-curricular projects;

- encourage a reflective-practitioner approach by clarifying the values, concepts and methods that are fundamental to various learning activities;

- help teachers and other educational staff to develop their own experiential learning projects, prompted by examples given in the reference book;

- increase the interest of policy makers, administrators, school governors, head teachers and classroom teachers in intercultural education as an efficient tool for addressing religious diversity in European schools, and in religious diversity as a means of supporting intercultural education.

PART I

THE THEORETICAL AND CONCEPTUAL BASIS FOR RELIGIOUS DIVERSITY AND INTERCULTURAL EDUCATION

1. The religious dimension in intercultural education

Micheline Milot

Introduction

Globalisation requires that education must rise to the challenges inherent in the growth of cultural and religious diversity in order to form citizens who are able to live together peacefully. Due attention paid to the religious dimension of intercultural education can make a significant contribution to peace, openness to other cultures, tolerance* and respect for human rights in Europe. Religious differences continue all too often to be a source of tension, conflict and discrimination.

What are we to understand by the "religious dimension" in intercultural education? In this section we shall clarify a number of fundamental considerations relating to the religious dimension and define some basic concepts. First we highlight a number of features of religion as a cultural phenomenon in our modern-day world. Then we ask in what form moral and religious convictions are to be found in the public sphere and at school, and how we can consider the religious dimension of intercultural education to help develop informed and peace-loving citizens who are open to intercultural dialogue. Finally we consider whether paying due attention to the religious dimension of intercultural education is compatible with a secular model of contemporary societies (with growing secularisation in some).

The diversity of beliefs and values and of identity-related claims based on religious affiliations, and the increasingly sensitive nature of freedom of conscience and religion, concern all democratic societies that have an interest in forming citizens capable of reflection and democratic participation. Our underlying idea is to approach religion, a social, cultural and political phenomenon, as a means of fostering democratic citizenship.

1. Religion as a cultural phenomenon

European societies have experienced a major process of secularisation in which the social and political importance of the Christian churches has clearly declined. The supernatural no longer dictates the political order of societies, but nonetheless, religious references are still to be found in a variety of forms in many groups and nations. In other words, whilst the major religious traditions no longer represent a force encompassing all aspects of political and social life, no public sphere is exempt from religion. For this reason, we can speak of religion as a "cultural phenomenon". Few currently doubt that secularisation is an irreversible feature of our societies, but it has to be acknowledged that it has not removed all traces of the religious experience and references from society. Such traces and references are found in diverse and new forms. Today, the symbols and values associated with the great religious traditions are still part of the collective memory. A broad majority of people in many countries still claim to belong to a particular religion (even though more often than not this does not necessarily imply that they are practising members). Secularisation has undoubtedly led to a narrowing of the social scope of traditional faiths. However, many new religious or spiritual groups have sprung up at the same time. The major migration flows which have had their impact on most societies have highlighted more clearly than in the past the diversity of ways of seeing life and the world, rooted in the different systems of belief. Many sporadic or endemic conflicts around the world involve groups that identify themselves with specific religious labels.

Two parallel processes are going on: on the one hand, individuals feel free to nurture a personal spirituality and subscribe to religious doctrines or take part in ritual practices without developing a sense of belonging to a particular group or faith; on the other, new religious movements attract a number of people seeking meaning or fellowship outside traditional forms of religion. Accordingly, what has been termed a "religious revival" is more an ongoing process of adaptation and acculturation of the ways in which human experience is imbued with a sacred dimension. In consequence, the very definition of religion goes far beyond a concept based on the great faiths.

In practice, the religious dimension is expressed through a number of social and political phenomena where the religious references of individuals play a major role: identity-based claims, manifestations of the distinctive features of a religion in the public arena, stances taken vis-à-vis political and moral issues in our societies, conflicts of standards between the freedom of conscience and religion and certain democratic values, such as gender equality. A further aspect of the new multifaceted context of the religious dimension is that it encompasses a wide variety of convictions, values and worldviews which are occasionally irreconcilable and at times a source of tension and discrimination between individuals and social groups.

Regardless of the way in which the religious dimension of life is reflected in the workings of society, it reminds us that the erosion of the political role of religions does not mean the end of the personal and social function of religious beliefs. While these may no longer determine the way the state is run, they nonetheless continue to play a key role which is not limited to the private sphere.

2. Moral, religious and philosophical convictions outside the private sphere

The erosion of the political power of traditional religions and the decrease in the impact of religion in the social sphere are two factors that have fuelled the process of secularisation over the last few decades. Religion has certainly survived, but has tended to withdraw into the private sphere. Theories of secularisation have often led to a simplistic interpretation of the place of religion in modern societies, equating the decline in traditional institutions with the "end of religion". Nonetheless, the modernist premise, coming from the Enlightenment, of the incompatibility between the irrational nature of religion and scientific rationality which supposedly governs modern societies has had to be re-evaluated in order to take account of the many forms of religious practice which continue to operate in society. In certain cases, religion can even become a vehicle for criticism of modern-day life, particularly, some of its shortcomings: excessive individualism and its impact on the sense of community, the lack of meaning, de-culturation brought about by globalisation and the erosion of the moral foundation of our societies.

Whilst religion has tended to become a matter of individual conscience, the social aspect of our lives has become increasingly more personalised. However, this does not imply that religion is confined solely to the private sphere and has nothing to do with the public arena. Moral and religious convictions underlie the motivation behind, and the nature of, social action. It is simply not the case that deeply felt convictions relate exclusively to one's private life whilst the public sphere becomes the stage for exchanges based on shared values and principles. Individuals take action, identify with each other socially, and adopt political positions in line with their values and beliefs, whether religious or philosophical. Moreover, moral and religious differences come to the fore precisely when they come into conflict with the values of other citizens in the political sphere.

Experience shows that social cohesion has little chance of developing if power relationships are left to govern social interactions of their own

accord, or if individuals are assumed to know automatically how to participate peacefully in public life with those who do not share their convictions.
Tolerance* and understanding are qualities which have to be learned.
States therefore have an interest in educating young people, most of whom
will have to live together in a given political context with (or despite) the
differences in their religious and moral outlooks. It is in this way that the
religious dimension has to be taken into account in intercultural education.

3. Manifestations of religious diversity in schools

School is without doubt one of the first places where children have daily
contact with the range of values and worldviews that shape individual
identities. Whether schools are secular, denominational or faith based, they
all share certain features:

- there is no real homogenous group of pupils, even within the same
  religious tradition, since religious practices and beliefs differ from one
  family to another and from one individual to another;

- in modern society there are different ways of conceiving what constitutes a "good" life, and these conceptions arise from various religious
  and non-religious views;

- children do not leave their values and deeply felt convictions outside
  when they enter the classroom. Neither children nor adults can be
  asked to abandon a large part of their identity in order to form a relationship with others.

Inevitably, therefore, the religious dimension of human experience is of
relevance to intercultural education as this dimension is a constituent part
of the culture and identity of a large number of individuals. Of course, the
values on which identity is based and moral preferences can also derive
from philosophical, humanist and agnostic convictions. Accordingly, the
term "religious dimension" in intercultural education is not used to refer to
some type of religious education, but is aimed primarily at fostering recip-
rocal awareness, respect, and learning how to live together in order to promote social cohesion and civic participation by all in a democratic context,
in which everyone feels accepted as an equal in terms of rights and
dignity.

There are manifestations of religious diversity in schools whatever their
type. One only has to think of the wearing of distinctive religious symbols
or ritual requirements (dietary or other) specific to certain religious groups.
However, the religious dimension goes far beyond these visible signs,

going right into the heart of the convictions and values which define individual and group identities.

Taking the religious dimension of intercultural education into account can be summarised as follows: intercultural education should ensure that it nurtures an understanding of the phenomena of both belief and non-belief and the ability to reflect on the different worldviews to be found in pluralist societies. It concerns the fundamental educational interests of children. These interests cover not only matters relating to general cognitive aptitudes but also a child's right to be prepared appropriately for life as a citizen playing a full part in democracy. Such education needs to develop personal autonomy and a critical spirit, tolerance,* openness to diversity and a feeling of belonging to the community as a whole. It should also nurture a sense of trust, uniting citizens beyond their moral and religious differences and disagreements. This approach to education may meet some resistance from some parents and teachers. For example, independence and critical-mindedness may offend the sensibilities of those believers who do not encourage such attitudes and of teachers who find it difficult to take account of people's beliefs if they feel they are a purely private matter. We believe nonetheless that the principles and approaches of this reference book will help to overcome these difficulties and foster a productive dialogue between all the different partners involved in children's education.

4. Citizenship, human rights and religious diversity

Any democratic state, even in highly secularised societies, is obliged to take a position vis-à-vis religious diversity. It has to handle its relations with the dominant faith communities which have for centuries shaped social, moral and even political life; it must then give consideration to minority groups anxious to preserve their traditions; it must also deal appropriately with the diversity of the many and varied group or individual demands regarding the public expression of freedom of conscience and religion.

At the same time, in all societies there is a discernible increase in awareness of human rights. International organisations exert increasingly greater pressure on states to ensure that they uphold fundamental rights. In addition, individuals are not happy to make do with rights on paper only; they want their rights to be upheld in practice. This concern in relation to fundamental rights (freedom of conscience and religion, freedom of expression, equality for everyone, etc.) is closely linked to a concept of citizenship which requires states to take the necessary steps to ensure that each citizen feels his or her dignity is respected and to promote social integration and participation.

Democratic states are expected to guarantee the paramount educational interests of children, which we have already looked at briefly. A key dimension of education is a child's right to be fully prepared for life as a citizen within a democratic and pluralist society. Citizens, however, must "live together" despite their moral and religious differences. Education should focus on developing abilities and attitudes which, in a manner of speaking, are the tools needed for the full exercise of citizenship. States need to encourage greater intercultural understanding and tolerance*. What contribution can intercultural education make to this?

5. Aims of the religious dimension in intercultural education

Bearing in mind the nature of the deeply felt convictions which define an individual's values and identity, how can intercultural education take account of the religious dimension so as to foster understanding, learning to live together, inclusion and participation? In our view there are three main aims of the religious dimension of intercultural education. These concern the principles of tolerance, reciprocity and civic-mindedness, and underlie a wide variety of educational activities and approaches to learning.

5.1. Tolerance

Tolerance is a concept which has given rise to a vast amount of literature. In short, tolerance can be understood in a "weak" or "strong" sense. In its weak sense, it equates quite simply to "tolerating", putting up with, from a distance, the fact that others may live as they wish even though they may not share our values or belong to the same cultural or religious group. Understood as such, tolerance allows for a (let us say) passive social peace-making process, but not necessarily respect for difference and the ability to discuss with those different from ourselves in the public arena. We can live in close proximity to and come into contact with others but without ever sharing anything with them. It is generally because the state "imposes" tolerance of this kind on the basis of legal constraints whereby individuals may not interfere with the freedom of those who adopt different values or lifestyles from their own.

Understood in a stronger sense, tolerance goes beyond mere resigned acceptance that others are entitled to the same freedom that we enjoy and which has been granted to us by the powers in government. It implies that we all may consider that our own convictions are true, good and valid for ourselves but that those of others are equally good and valid in their eyes and that it is not for us to pass judgement on their conception of what constitutes a "good life". This is a long and gradual learning process, particularly when it comes to religious convictions which are based on absolutes and not on any social consensus which is always liable to review and reappraisal. Children cannot learn tolerance in this strong sense unless they are exposed to points of view that differ from those they learn from their family or the religious group to which they belong.

This aim can be subdivided into two objectives. The first is an awareness of various life options, not only to improve one's general culture, but also to nurture respect for others. Moral and religious diversity is undeniably a sociological variable which makes it essential to be aware of the constituent parts of a social landscape which is no longer homogenous (although, in point of fact, it has never been totally so). But in order to promote intercultural understanding it is not enough for children simply to be taught the multitude of beliefs and religious practices that exist. Awareness of the beliefs of others does not necessarily lead to tolerance. There is even a risk that divisions will become more acute if the spotlight is focused on the vast array of different moral and religious convictions. So awareness of different moral and religious convictions, albeit necessary, must serve a second objective: that of respect for others as having equal dignity. In terms of intercultural education, respect for the difference of others therefore goes far beyond mere awareness. It is more importantly a matter of developing a respectful attitude towards others, enabling them to feel accepted as they are. It also involves learning to live without feeling under threat because of one's differences. The goal is to promote an ability to understand the point of view of people with different religious or philosophical convictions.

Enhanced awareness of the religious dimension should be aimed at ensuring that each child, to whatever extent he or she identifies with a particular religious group, is able to acquire a positive sense of identity, without fear of being judged by others. The more a group feels marginalised socially because of its beliefs or the way such beliefs are publicly expressed, the more frequently it resorts to aggressive or defensive withdrawal strategies, at the expense of civic participation. This also holds good for people who identify with a majority group within society: learning to acknowledge others should avoid developing a "majority reflex", which more often than not is condescending and can result in considerable discrimination through fear of difference.

5.2. Reciprocity

The ability to think in terms of reciprocity is a social skill comprising a readiness to acknowledge or grant others the same things one would like to see recognised or granted for oneself and not to offend others on matters on which one would not wish to be offended oneself (the same principle applies to an unbelieving child vis-à-vis a child who is a devout believer). This leads into the ethics of social relations. Education should help children develop the ability to distinguish between the legitimacy of their conception of what is good and true and their attitude towards those who do not share the same view. Young people should be able to assess what they can expect from others who do not share the same values and convictions. Ultimately this should encourage citizens to feel able to participate in public debate on the grounds of their religious convictions with such participation being judged valid in the eyes of others. As reciprocity cannot be defined by laws or regulations, it presupposes an education process.

While children are rarely expected to take part in public debate, readiness to do so is acquired through a slow process of education and socialisation. Indeed, this process begins at a very young age in the school yard, since, aside from the home, this is one of the first environments where acceptance of difference and respect for others need to be put into effect and where the slightest deviation from the "norm" can so easily lead to a child becoming marginalised vis-à-vis other pupils.

5.3. Civic-mindedness

Character traits which make it possible to show respect for others and conceive our social relations in terms of reciprocity are reflected in practice in the public sphere by an attitude which could be termed as a sense of civic responsibility. The first meaning of this concept relates to a citizen's attitude in public life. It does not refer to a regulatory ideal, but a means of co-existence which will bring about both respect and reciprocity. Both of these presuppose a capacity for reflection and a certain moderation in the public expression of one's convictions. In the literal sense, which is the one we typically find in dictionaries, the capacity for reflection is the capacity to have thought focus on itself. It presupposes an ability to distance oneself from one's own convictions and beliefs. So many conflicts come about by the blindfolded adherence to absolute convictions. In considering the religious dimension, what exactly is a sense of civic responsibility? What criteria could we use to reference book us in our definition? While the recognition of freedom of conscience, religion and expression always comes with certain limits attached, the absolute nature of religious declarations can constitute an obstacle to respect for others and lead to unequal treatment of those who do not share those beliefs.

a. A capacity to stand back

The ability to stand back with regard to one's own moral or religious convictions does not equate with denying them nor is it the same as adopting a relativist attitude. Neither is it a matter of requiring children to make value judgements on the beliefs to which they and their families subscribe. A capacity for reflection must not be confused with a radical criticism of traditional norms, nor with an implicit desire to tear down the foundations on which identity is based. Uprooting specific cultures is most certainly not a desirable aim. While the capacity for reflection does involve a certain ability for distancing oneself from the values and beliefs to which one subscribes, its objective is not cultural uprooting but rather the development of a cognitive ability which is in harmony with the objectives of intercultural education, in other words the ability for openness to others with due regard for their dignity.

It is normal for children to be introduced to the traditional beliefs of the group to which they belong, in the family or, for example, when attending church, the mosque or any other place of worship. At school, however, it is not unreasonable to expect children to develop a capacity for distance, simply by becoming aware that that identification makes sense for them and those around them who subscribe to the same views, whereas other children may legitimately have other beliefs or believe in some other manner. Without this capacity for distancing, neither children nor adults can understand how different absolute statements can be equally legitimate. This capacity for distance clearly introduces a degree of relativity as regards moral and religious options, but relativity should not be confused with relativism. While relativism tends to bring moral preferences down to the same level, holding that they are equally valid, a sense of relativity simply induces one to acknowledge that convictions are always valid from a particular point of view, in particular that of the community that holds them.

This is a gradual learning process which undoubtedly is easier for children than for adults. Once again, the school needs to be given a role which is different from, albeit complementary to, that of the family and religious organisations. Furthermore, this distancing from religious convictions is generally speaking not offensive for children and parents, since it is not, strictly speaking, critical in nature, but rather primarily cognitive.

b.   Moderation in the public expression of identity

The second civic attitude is moderation concerning the social affirmation of one's identity and convictions. Moderation does not mean that one must repress or conceal one's religious identity, but rather that it should be expressed in a way that does not impede mutual respect and sharing with others. As pointed out above, this goes beyond the threshold of tolerance in the "weak sense".

Certain strong and "exclusive" forms of affirmation may have a place within the family circle or group to which one belongs, but insofar as such forms may lead to discrimination and the unfair treatment of others, moderation means that individuals should adopt a sort of inner "code of public life" so that they can establish respectful and collaborative relationships with others. This attitude does not concern only those people belonging to minority groups whose religious convictions largely define their social identity and play a major role in their moral decisions. It also applies to majority groups that, even in a broadly secularised state, often develop expectations with respect to those of their fellow citizens who fit a different profile. These expectations are geared towards ensuring that the latter's behaviour within civil society is consistent with the general, often implicit, rules of the majority.

Once again, this moderation is not something that develops spontaneously on reaching adulthood. It must be taught as an integral part of the objectives of intercultural education. Schools must seek to kindle mutual respect among young people so that everyone can live in accordance with their convictions while recognising that they have to set certain limits to the expression of those convictions in their relationships with other people. To accomplish this, the above-mentioned criteria must be applied: as soon as children are confident that their specific identities are recognised as legitimate within the school, and when they have access, through learning, to the tools they need to develop their thinking skills, moderation will not be perceived as being self-denial but a way of relating to others who do not share the same convictions.

6. The religious dimension and secular society

Is consideration of the religious dimension of intercultural education compatible with the secular nature of many public institutions, political neutrality or a high level of secularisation of education in general?

First of all, democracies are, to varying degrees and in different ways, largely secular societies. Such a statement must, however, be qualified. For example, the French form of secularism *(laïcité)* represents a way of managing relationships between churches and the state, but the underlying political and legal principles involved are found in other democratic contexts. There is no such thing as "pure secularity", nor would a purely secular society be in any way desirable. Given the complexity of today's societies and the current models of church–state relationships shaped by national traditions, political and legal bodies have to adopt a progressive attitude towards religion which is itself evolving. Such an adaptation to pluralism presupposes on the part of democracies an ability to combine a conception of the cultural, historically discrete nation with a conception of the civic, multi-ethnic nation. Political neutrality does not mean that the state must ignore the fact that citizens gear their social and political actions to their beliefs. However, it does mean that the state must be scrupulous in safeguarding its citizens' freedom of conscience and religion, and ensuring that it does not put any particular religious group at an advantage or disadvantage.

Secularisation is a process that has to make room for a wide range of questions raised by cultural and religious diversity. Secularism does not constitute a threat to religion and religion is no longer a threat to secularism. Nonetheless, there is always a risk that the religious dimension in intercultural education might offend the sensitivities of believers and non-believers: for the former, the fear that their convictions will become trivialised and relativised, and for the latter the fear of disguised proselytism or greater emphasis placed on human credulity. Moreover, in several countries, the religious dimension is viewed, historically, as belonging exclusively to the private sphere (for example family, faith community or religious teaching in denominational schools).

Whatever form the secular system or rule of law takes in any given national context, political neutrality must find ways of integrating diversity, respect for cultural traditions and dialogue between people with due regard for fundamental rights. This concerns our ability to live together. Secular and secularised societies must offer a framework that allows for the recognition of diversity in a society of equal citizens, free from all discrimination with regard to their personal choices in matters of belief. This recognition is a necessity and a prerequisite for defining shared standards in a pluralist context. Common standards cannot be defined once and for all; rather they are the fruit of interaction and dialogue in a multicultural context. Education has a fundamental role to play to ensure that intercultural understanding can foster harmonious co-existence and tolerance.

**Key points of the religious dimension
of intercultural education**

- Religion must be understood as a social, cultural and political phenomenon in modern secular societies.

- Religion is not confined solely to the private sphere, away from the public arena: moral and religious convictions underlie motivation and the nature of social action.

- It is important that states safeguard citizens' freedom of religion and conscience.

- Manifestations of religious diversity in schools include visible symbols and requirements and invisible convictions and values.

- Intercultural education should ensure an understanding of the different world views found in pluralist societies.

- Intercultural education needs to develop personal autonomy, a critical spirit, openness to diversity, and a feeling of belonging to the community as a whole, as well as nurture a sense of trust, uniting citizens beyond their moral and religious differences, in order to play a full part in democracy.

- The aims of the religious dimension of intercultural education are to promote:

    o tolerance: awareness of various life options and respect for others;

    o reciprocity: a readiness to acknowledge or grant others the same things one would like to see recognised or granted for oneself, and not to offend others on matters on which one would not wish to be offended oneself;

    o civic-mindedness: ability to stand back with capacity for reflection and moderation in the public expression of identity, with mutual respect and sharing with others.

Robert Jackson

Introduction

This section discusses some key concepts relating to the study of religious diversity within intercultural education. The view is taken that religion should not be studied in isolation, but in the context of other social categories, such as culture, race and nationality and against the wider general debate about pluralism. None of these concepts can be defined straightforwardly. All of them are subject to on-going debates. Educational approaches to religious diversity should introduce students to the debates at their own level.

1. Plurality

All European societies exhibit some degree of diversity or plurality in the spheres of religions, values and culture. First, there is the plurality that corresponds to the observable cultural diversity present in many western societies, usually resulting from the migration of peoples or, in certain cases, the presence of indigenous peoples (as with the Sami in Norway). In the case of Britain, especially since the early 1950s, migrants moved from South Asia, East Africa and the Caribbean, bringing significant numbers with, for example, Muslim, Hindu and Sikh family backgrounds and minorities of other backgrounds such as Pentecostal Christian and Rastafarian. To give another example, before end of the 1960s, Norway had relatively few immigrants. Then there was an influx of Pakistani migrants, a typical labour-seeking chain migration, similar in character to the migration of Pakistanis to Britain and elsewhere in Europe. There are also minority migrant populations from Vietnam and the former Yugoslavia in Norway. To take a third example, France, like Britain, has migrants from former colonies, in this case from North Africa (Algeria, then Morocco and Tunisia), and from African states further south. Most of these migrants are Muslim by religion. France also has migrants of a Catholic background from European countries such as Portugal and Spain. The emergence of new religious movements and various new age phenomena can also be seen as yet another aspect of the religious plurality of western societies. This form of plurality, which draws attention to different groups within society, has been called "traditional plurality" (Skeie 1995).

Another form of plurality reflects the fact that, in contemporary western societies, individuals are often in a position to choose values and ideas from a variety of sources. Individuals may reject religions and their claims, for example, and base their values on some form of non-religious philosophy such as secular humanism. Others might synthesise beliefs and values from religious and humanistic sources. In the context of religion, individuals might describe themselves as being from a particular religious background, but cease to hold some of the religious beliefs that orthodox believers hold. Thus, for example, a post-modern Christian might see the religion more as a spiritual and ethical way of life rather than a traditional system of belief. It is not uncommon to find individuals valuing some or other form of spirituality, while rejecting traditional religious beliefs. Such individuals might make their own personal synthesis of ideas from different religious and spiritual sources, just as they might utilise a range of cultural ideas and practices. This form of plurality has sometimes been called "modern" or "post-modern plurality" (Skeie 1995).

It is important to note the intertwined relationship between traditional and modern/post-modern plurality. Thus, changes and developments within a religious tradition – for example changes in religious belief and practice across the generations – have to be seen not just in terms of traditional plurality, but under influences from modern/post-modern plurality. When studied "in the field", so to speak, religions can be seen to encompass some variety of belief, practice and cultural expression. Attention to modern/post-modern plurality accentuates this diversity within religions even more and blurs their edges. In studying religions, it is clear that this diversity needs to be taken into account in order to avoid stereotyping.

2. Plurality and pluralism

So far, we have used the term "plurality" as a descriptive term. Some writers distinguish between "plurality" in this descriptive sense and "pluralism" as a normative idea. Perhaps everyone can agree, in a descriptive sense, that there is plurality. However, the view that different individuals take on defining and interpreting that plurality represents their own particular views in the debate about pluralism. This way of looking at plurality and pluralism helps in the analysis of key concepts that relate to religion in society, such as culture, ethnicity and nationality. The debates show a range of positions.

At one extreme there are "closed" views that define the concepts very specifically and picture religions as homogeneous systems. At the other, there are post-modern views that offer complete deconstructions of "religions" and "cultures". According to this view "religions" and "cultures" are artificial constructions that serve the interests of particular groups of people. There are many possible positions between these two extremes.

The key educational task is to engage learners, over the years of schooling, in a critical analysis of how such ideas are used, both with regard to examples from religion, especially in relation to its social context, and in relation to their own experience. By participating in such discussions, students can learn about different stances on religion or culture, but can also examine their own and their peers' assumptions and gradually formulate and clarify their own views. This form of education goes beyond simply giving information about different religions, and engages students in the democratic context of the school. Different positions within the debates can be used to clarify, challenge or illuminate different points of view, some of which may be suggested by students. Obviously, the precise content of studies that deal with these issues, and the methods used, will depend on the age and aptitude of children and young people and on other contextual factors. These include the particular history of religion and state in their own country, and the related pattern of civil religion within their own society.

3. Stereotyping

A key principle of the study of religious diversity in the context of plurality described above is the avoidance of stereotyping. The term was introduced by the French printer Didot in 1789 for the plates used in printing, was later used metaphorically by psychiatrists and by Pavlov in his experiments, and then became used more generally in the social sciences. Stereotypes are overgeneralisations (often erroneous and oversimplifying), often about people or groups, based on assumptions and misinformation rather than on facts. Stereotypes do not take account of the enormous diversity of the people belonging to a given group. They do not consider the current circumstances of the individual or the range of reasons why members of a group or category may differ from one another in a variety of ways. Stereotypes can lead to discriminatory behaviour, and often serve to justify prejudice. The approaches to religions, cultures, ethnicity and nationality that are introduced below aim to avoid stereotyping.

4. Religions

One key question for those introducing the study of religious diversity is "What 'are' religions?" There are no straightforward answers to this question and, in addressing it as teachers or students, we enter a debate rather than find clear-cut solutions that everyone will agree upon. In relation to intercultural education and anti-racism, the question about the nature of religions is very important, since these fields aim to counter stereotyping of all kinds.

The most conservative views picture religions as clearly distinct systems of belief. Individuals who belong to a particular religion are portrayed as having a clear set of beliefs and practices that they share with others from the same background. However, if we look from the point of view of groups or individual people rather than total religious systems, we get a different picture. First, if we look at religious groups or at individuals, we are likely to find considerable diversity within the framework of any religion – whether denominational, sectarian or cultural, or composed of some combination of these categories. Secondly, many individuals may have a personal philosophy or spirituality that uses ideas from a variety of sources – some of which may be from inside and others from outside a particular religion – or makes a new interpretation of traditional ideas. The descriptive reality, as reflected in field studies of religions conducted by anthropologists and other social scientists, reveals complex patterns of belief, practice and cultural influence that defy any simple classification.

At various points in history, often at times of conflict, some religious believers have tended to stereotype other religions. However, the modern tendency to portray religions as distinct intellectual belief systems was influenced by the rationalism of 18th-century Europe, and also by the encounter of religions and cultures through colonialism. As writers such as Edward Said have pointed out, the more powerful European colonialists were in a position to compare their understanding of other beliefs and practices with their own formalised understanding of Christianity (Said 1978). For example, until the 18th century, when the British and other colonialists went to India, there was no such concept as "Hindu religion". It was westerners who introduced this idea to distinguish the mass of diverse devotional practice to be found in India that was not Islam, Christianity or Judaism. By the early 19th century the word "Hinduism" was coined, by an Irish soldier, writing from India about Indian religion for an audience in Britain. Terms such as Buddhism and Sikhism also emerged in the 19th century. The words were taken up by practitioners, and also by students of the new discipline of comparative religion, and they are still dominant in European text-books.

One problem with looking at religions in this way is that it lends itself to stereotyping. It is easy to assume that each religion has a set of fixed beliefs on which all insiders are expected to agree. Any study of religion in every-day life would reveal that this is not the case. From the point of view of teaching and learning about religious diversity, we need pedagogical models that resist stereotyping and allow for differences within religious traditions to be expressed and understood. In the next section of the book, we will look at some pedagogical approaches that might be used in study-ing religious diversity. For example, the interpretive approach portrays reli-gions dynamically and encourages a flexible approach to learning that avoids stereotyping (Jackson 1997, 2004c, 2005b, 2005c). Instead of repre-senting religions simply as belief systems, this model portrays a "religion" in terms of a dynamic relationship between individuals, the groups they iden-tify with (sectarian, denominational, ethnic, cultural, etc.) and a broadly described religious tradition. This approach does not deny that there are religions, but reveals the diversity and complexity of religious traditions and the different ways in which the term "religion" is used. The approach has been used successfully with young children (Barratt 1994a, b, c, d, e) as well as with adolescents (Mercier 1996, Robson 1995, Wayne *et al.* 1996).

5. Culture and cultures

There is an on-going debate about the relationship between religion and culture that is reflected in discussions of religions in European societies, so it is important to consider the concepts of culture and cultures when pre-paring to teach about religions. If we look historically at the term "culture", then, in the 15th century, we find it referring to the tending of crops or to rearing animals. During the next two centuries it is used, by analogy, to refer to the human mind. During the 18th century, "culture" became asso-ciated with the arts and scholarship – in philosophy and history, for example – and was considered to be for the wealthy.[2] At about the same time, under the influence of the German philosopher Herder, we get an alternative view, namely the idea of distinct and variable cultures, a view developed in the Romantic Movement. A generalised or "essentialised" culture was regarded as the collective "heritage" of the national group and identified with a particular ethnic group.

2. During the 20th century, the term "popular culture" emerged – mass culture working through the mass media – a notion in tension with "high culture" (that is, the 18th-century "high arts" idea of culture).

This closed view of cultures came into early social or cultural anthropology. Ruth Benedict, for example, compares cultures to different types of living organism, seeing them as clearly distinct from one another. For Benedict, cultures either survived or died out, with no possibility of the formation of new cultural expressions through cultural interaction (Benedict 1935). The idea of uniform, completely distinct cultures was perpetuated in early work in multicultural education in Britain and is still to be found, for example, in the rhetoric of the political far right and in some popular newspapers in different European countries.

At the opposite extreme there are post-modern deconstructions of the idea of "a culture", with any idea of continuous tradition being regarded as a "meta-narrative", a distorted account invented in their own interests by those with power. On this view, the way of life someone adopts is a matter of personal, individual choice. In between the two poles are intermediary positions, emphasising the changing and contested nature of cultures over time. One of these is Clifford Geertz's view of cultures as internally diverse, but with cultural continuity maintained through inherited ideas, and expressed through particular symbols (Geertz 1973, p. 89). Another position, reflected in the work of James Clifford (1986) and Edward Said (1978), emphasises internal (sometimes inter-generational) conflict or negotiation in creating cultural change over time. This latter position also draws attention to the role of the observer (whether anthropologist, historian, journalist or student) in constructing "cultures". On this view, as with biographies, single definitive accounts of a culture are not possible. Accounts of a culture are "better" or "worse".

There are also those who emphasise process rather than content in making and describing culture. Culture is seen not so much as an "object", but as an active process through which humans produce change. Instead of having a distinct and fixed cultural identity, individuals and groups identify with elements of culture, or create new culture through bringing different elements together. The emphasis is on people engaging with culture, making use of different cultural resources (for example Østberg 2003). The emphasis in identity formation is less on descent and inheritance, and more on a series of identifications through dialogue and communication with others.

6. Cultural discourse

Field research studies by social scientists confirm that there are both inflexible and highly flexible approaches to nationality, ethnicity, religion and their relationship in discourse about culture (Baumann 1999). In various situations, there are those whose interests might be to present a particular relationship between a fixed view of culture (or cultures) and reified or abstracted views of nationality, ethnicity and religion. Thus, British national identity is often described by the political far right as if it were some kind of fixed entity (often associated romantically with terms like "Anglo-Saxon"), with its own distinct culture, related to a closed view of ethnicity (usually with "Britishness" being associated with being white), and religion (Christianity in very particular forms). Similar patterns may be found in other European states. Such closed views provide simplistic criteria for judging whether someone is "truly" British, French, German or whatever. Similarly, both outsiders and insiders might use terminology such as "the Muslim community" or "Asian culture" when it suits their purposes. The German anthropologist Gerd Baumann calls this tendency to reify – to treat an abstract idea as though it were a concrete reality – "dominant discourse". "Dominant discourse" is often used by extremist groups, politicians, the media and sometimes by cultural communities themselves. Baumann distinguishes this from "demotic discourse", the language of culture making, which often becomes used when people from various different backgrounds interact in discussing issues of common concern or engaging in projects of mutual interest. Baumann's conclusion is that "culture" can be seen as both a possession of an ethnic or religious "community", and also as a dynamic process relying on personal choice, in which, for example, community boundaries may be renegotiated (Baumann 1996).

7. Multicultural societies

The term "multicultural" is often used narrowly, to convey the simple and inaccurate idea of completely distinct and separate cultures present within a single society. Some views of multicultural education, for example, picture cultures as distinct traditions, with minority cultures functioning in their own private space, and depending on the values of the dominant culture for their continued existence. Evidence from field research shows that this idea of a multicultural society does not correspond to real life experience. This is one of the reasons why many writers prefer the term "intercultural". However, as with the expression "intercultural", the term "multicultural" can be used very flexibly.

In the case of the term "multicultural", its use in the context of society needs to acknowledge both "dominant" and "demotic" forms of discourse. The way we picture a multicultural society needs to be flexible. Not only are the boundaries between groups unclear, but minority cultures, religions and ethnicities are themselves internally pluralistic, and the symbols and values of their various constituent groups are open to negotiation, contest and change. Moreover, individuals from any background may identify with values associated with a range of sources and may draw eclectically on a variety of resources in creating new culture. A young person might be a "skilled cultural navigator" (Ballard 1994) or display "multiple cultural competence" (Jackson and Nesbitt 1993). At the same time, in the context of groups, there will be those claiming a more bounded religious and cultural identity. Thus a multicultural society is not a patchwork of several fixed cultural identities, but "an elastic web of crosscutting and always mutually situational identifications" (Baumann 1999, p. 118). Of crucial importance for the maintenance and development of such societies is the provision of educational strategies that raise awareness of the debates and foster dialogue and communication. Educational strategies need to identify common or overlapping ideas and values, but they also must identify and address difference. Such interactions promote intercultural understanding.

8. Ethnicity

In the context of a discussion of religious diversity, it is important to examine the terms "ethnicity" and related words, since these are often closely connected with religious identity in their use. The term "Hinduism", for example, is often associated with people of Indian ethnic ancestry, even though they might not be Indian by nationality.

The word ethnic – derived from *ethnos*, the Greek word for "people" – is in common usage in English and has equivalents in some other European languages. A teacher thinking of moving to a new job might ask "What is the ethnic mix in the school? Which ethnic groups are represented?" In reporting the civil war in the former Yugoslavia journalists used the chilling term "ethnic cleansing" for the first time. In these various cases, "ethnic" refers to groups, which, in principle, can interact with one another. Ethnicity can also refer to categories, for example in classifying members of a particular population by skin colour or by some other general category such as "Asian" or "Caucasian". As with "race" and "culture", "ethnicity" can be stereotyped in order to separate and isolate groups. It is therefore a term that needs to be used with caution.

Ethnic groups are popularly thought of as having a common ancestry and descent, marked by some form of cultural continuity which distinguishes them from other groups around them. There is also the common identification of supposedly overt "racial" difference and ethnic difference. Ethnic differences can also be highlighted by legal definition, as in a legal judgment made in England in 1983, in which Sikhs were ruled to be an ethnic group (Jones and Welengama 2000, p. 40).

If a person is labelled as being from a certain ethnic group, then that person can be stereotyped by certain "outsiders" or members of the majority culture, "locked" into a particular identity that they may feel they do not have and expected to behave in certain preconceived ways. "Insiders" might also sometimes have an interest in presenting a closed view of their own ethnic group. This static view has been criticised especially by those who have recognised the situational character of ethnicity through their field research. Thus, the Norwegian researcher Fredrik Barth draws attention to changes that take place across socially constructed ethnic boundaries, where one group influences another, either positively or negatively (Barth 1969). Such ethnic re-formation takes place, for example, among groups which have rediscovered religious or ethnic symbols as a result of being marginalised by more powerful groups around them, or groups that have attempted to redefine themselves in response to influences or pressures from other social groups or institutions. Barth's analysis of ethnicity focuses attention on the maintenance of ethnic boundaries. Ethnic identity is not fixed, but is defined situationally.

In her research on Pakistani Muslim young people in Britain, Jessica Jacobson highlights this shifting nature of ethnic identity. Jacobson observed that a sense of ethnic identity can vary according to context. It could be more related to a Pakistani ancestry or be "British Pakistani" in certain contexts (in the family, for example), and be "Asian" or "British Asian" in another (with members of the peer group, for example). Jacobson's research suggests that, in the case of young British Pakistani Muslims, there is evidence that ethnicity is in a state of flux and rapid change, while religion is perceived as stable and having universal applicability (Jacobson 1997). Parallel results were found in Sissel Østberg's study of Pakistani Muslim children in Oslo in which she found young people identifying with local places and traditions in Norway and Pakistan in forming their own "integrated plural identities" (Østberg 2003).

Some writers also speak of "hyphenated" ethnic identities. For example, Michael Fischer's analysis of "Chinese-American" ethnic identity finds a group with an ancestry that goes ultimately to China (so there is still some sense of ancestry). However, he also asserts that ethnicity is dynamic, and not taught and learned, not simply passed on from generation to generation. To be Chinese-American "... is a matter of finding a voice or style that does not violate one's several components of identity" (Fischer 1986,

p. 196). Shared ancestry is still an ingredient of ethnicity, but the internal variety within an ethnic group is acknowledged, as well as an element of creativity through which individuals attempt to express their "integrated plural identity".

The most radical positions in the debate reject the very idea of ethnicity. These include forms of nationalism in which ethnic and cultural distinctions are assimilated, such as the "melting pot" view of society in which differences are eradicated – hence the image of different metals being heated together in the same vessel until they melt and merge into one single alloy. Another such view is the post-modernist position, which sees ethnicity as an oppressive social construction. On this last view, even the situational analysis of ethnicity, with its use of terms such as "group", "boundary" and "maintenance", is regarded as potentially enclosing individuals within artificial identities.

Many field studies find that "ethnicity" implies some degree of identification with an ancestral tradition or a sense of "shared peoplehood" (Dashefsky 1972). However, ethnicity also changes situationally, includes an element of cultural choice and can never be fixed or static (Jackson and Nesbitt 1993). As Gerd Baumann puts it, "Both wine and ethnicity are … creations of human minds, skills and plans – based on some natural ingredients it is true, but far beyond anything that nature could do by itself" (Baumann 1999, p. 64).

9. The nation-state and nationality

The concepts of the nation-state and of nationalism are also relevant to educational discussions of religious diversity, for there are those who associate a particular state and its values and traditions with only one particular religion, while others would take a much broader view.

Nationalism is the ideology of one or more privileged ethnic groups or categories, who regard an "essentialised" and romanticised culture as the "heritage" of the national group. Inflexible and narrow views of national, ethnic and religious identity tend to emerge when fixed views of the nature of cultures are combined with reified views of nationality, ethnicity and religion. Nationalism leads both to "biological racism" and to what Tariq Modood calls "cultural racism". Cultural racism builds on biological racism in order to vilify cultural difference (Modood 1997). (See below on race and racism.)

However, some nation-states attempt to find ways of incorporating more than one ethnic group through abstracting a romantic idea of "super-ethnicity", with ideas such as "the American people" or the idea of assimilation through a "melting pot" of cultures. Perhaps this view is evident in some French policies with regard to culture in the public domain. This notion is in tension with any idea of retaining the distinctive but shifting cultural traditions of minorities.

Another way of accommodating ethnic or religious difference is through finding ways to incorporate different groups through the modification of civil religion or national custom. In Britain, for example, there is a gradual incorporation of the main faiths represented in the country into national and local civic religious life – whether a royal wedding or funeral, a mayoral investiture or hospital or prison chaplaincy (Beckford and Gilliat 1998). The current British heir to the throne's declaration that he does not see himself as the future "Defender of the Faith", but as a "defender of faith" is another example. A further example comes from Germany, where there is no state church. State and religious communities are independent. Legal status of religious communities as public corporations is guaranteed by article 137 of the basic constitutional law. This is the case for the Roman Catholic Church, the Protestant Church in Germany (EKD) (a network of 26 regional Protestant churches) as well as for many smaller religious communities and worldviews. There is a current debate about how far Islamic communities can fulfil the requirements to be acknowledged as a public corporation. What is clear from reflections on civil religion is that each nation-state has its own variety, conditioned by its own particular history. In this sense the nation-state cannot be entirely neutral when dealing with issues of religious and cultural diversity.

Whatever the difficulties, it is crucial that members of different minorities need to be involved directly in the democratic processes of society. Different views as to how this goal might be achieved vary according to the degree to which religions, ethnic groups and cultures are regarded as internally homogeneous. Those taking a "closed" view (and they might be insiders as well as outsiders) tend to take the line that "representatives" can speak authoritatively on behalf of their constituencies, while those emphasising the varied and contested nature of groups look for a much wider range of activities through which many different individuals (including women and children) can participate in dialogue and negotiation with others.

10. "Race" and "racism"

The concepts of "race" and "racism" are also highly relevant to discussions of education about religious diversity. "Race" is a scientifically discredited term used in the past to describe what were believed to be biologically distinct groups of human beings. "Racism" (or "biological racism") refers to discrimination against others on the basis of their supposed membership of a "racial" group. Many writers on racism agree that the essence of racism is the belief that there is a strong relationship between the membership of a social category (for example a "cultural" or "religious" group) and the possession of certain characteristics (such as skin colour). Thus the underlying explanation of "racial" differences may be cultural or religious, for example, and not "biological". Some writers use the term "cultural racism" to emphasise this association of appearance with a stereotyped view of a culture or religion (Modood 1997).

Another form of racism is "institutional racism". This has been defined as:

> The collective failure of an organization to provide an appropriate and professional service to people because of their colour, culture or ethnic origin which can be seen or detected in processes; attitudes and behaviour which amount to discrimination through unwitting prejudice, ignorance, thoughtlessness and racist stereotyping which disadvantages minority ethnic people [The Macpherson Report].[3]

Organisations such as the police, health, and education services, need to be aware of the dangers of unconscious institutional racism in their procedures. In schools these might relate to admissions procedures, school policies on racism and the extent that a school values religious diversity and difference, or makes parents from religious or ethnic minorities feel welcome in the school.

11. Anti-racism, multiculturalism and intercultural education

Since the 1970s some writers in Britain who described themselves as anti-racists were very critical of multicultural education because so much of it dealt with stereotypical (see "stereotyping" above) or generalised ideas of cultures and religions. This form of multiculturalism was seen, unintentionally, to reinforce racism (Jackson 2004a, b, d, 2005b). Recent work in intercultural and multicultural education has been much more aware of the debates about culture and identity. Many writers no longer separate the two areas of anti-racism and multiculturalism, seeing the two as complementary. Anti-racists, who used to write mainly about changing structures

---

3. http://www.archive.official-documents.co.uk/document/cm42/4262/4262.htm

of power in society in order to create justice for everyone, now are also concerned with issues of culture.

As noted above, many educators prefer to use the term intercultural education rather than multicultural education in order to emphasise a more critical and interactive view of culture than that used in early multicultural education. This is the view taken, for example, in the European journal *Intercultural Education*. As the Swiss writer Micheline Rey puts it,

> Regardless of the context in which it is used, the word "intercultural", precisely because it contains the prefix "inter", necessarily implies: interaction, exchange, desegregation, reciprocity, interdependence and solidarity. As it also contains the word "culture", it further denotes in its fullest sense: recognition of the values, lifestyles and symbolic conceptions to which human beings, both as individuals and in groups, refer in their dealings with others and in their vision of the world, as well as recognition of the interactions occurring both between the multiple registers of one and the same culture and between the various cultures in space and time (Rey 1991, 142).

Conclusion

A consideration of the above concepts helps us to see that the terminology needs to be used precisely, as much in teaching and learning as in any other context, and with some explanation where necessary. Terms such as "religious" and "ethnic" can be used very narrowly and exclusively, but not necessarily so. For example, the term "multicultural" is sometimes used by politicians in a pejorative way, to mean a society made up of different and more or less exclusive cultural groups. We have seen that the term can also be used much more flexibly. Similarly, some politicians use the term "integration", when they really mean "assimilation". The key point is to make clear one's use of the terminology and to help learners to look at others' uses of terms such as "religion", "multicultural society", "ethnic", "culture" and "integration" critically. Familiarity with the use of relevant language can help both educators and students to appreciate that a multicultural society can be seen, not as a collection of discrete and sometimes incompatible cultures, but as one in which cross-cutting religious, cultural and ethnic differences are acknowledged in a spirit of tolerance within a common, integrated democratic framework.

Key points of religious and cultural diversity: some key concepts

A distinction should be made between plurality and pluralism.

Religion should not be studied in isolation, but in the context of other social categories, such as culture, race and nationality and against the wider general debate about pluralism.

One problem with looking at religions or belief systems in this way is that it lends itself to stereotyping. It is easy to assume that each religion has a set of fixed beliefs on which all insiders are expected to agree.

The interpretive approach portrays religions dynamically and encourages a flexible approach to learning that avoids stereotyping. Instead of representing religions simply as belief systems, this model portrays a "religion" in terms of a dynamic relationship between individuals, the groups they identify with (sectarian, denominational, ethnic, cultural, etc.) and a broadly described religious tradition.

There are important distinctions in meaning between culture, cultures and cultural discourse.

The term multicultural is often variously used. Recent work in intercultural and multicultural education has been much more aware of the on-going debates within academic circles about culture and identity.

There are important distinctions in meaning between ethnicity, nationality, nationalism, race, racism, anti-racism and multiculturalism.

It is important to use terminology precisely and critically.

PART II

EDUCATIONAL CONDITIONS AND METHODOLOGICAL APPROACHES

Introduction

Peter Schreiner

This section introduces useful approaches and considers methodological issues concerning intercultural education that take account of religious diversity. Awareness of and sensibility to religious diversity in any society involves many different aspects. Internal policies, social security systems, community relations and ways to organise day-to-day life are influenced by the fact of religious diversity. Dealing with religious diversity in a fruitful way cannot be limited to public education. However, intercultural education, as a specific approach to cultural differences, may enable us better to face the challenges of religious diversity in European societies today. In the first part of this reference book the following principles have already been presented: tolerance, including respect for others; reciprocity as an important thinking and social skill; and civic attitudes, such as an ability to stand back and capacity for reflection, and moderation in the public expression of one's own identity with due regard for others' dignity.

These principles are fundamental to this section of the reference book, but they are not exclusive. Other factors can play a role as well when it comes to organising the teaching and learning process in the classroom. Not all methodologies have the same value in the different contexts. They have to be linked up to the varying education systems in different societies.

It has already been made clear that the fact of religious diversity in Europe cannot be ignored, and cannot be limited to the private sphere. Religious convictions shape personal and collective conceptions of beauty and justice, definitions of right and wrong, and perceptions of the past and of the future. The ambiguous face of religion has also been mentioned already. Intercultural education should encourage a reflective and sensitive encounter with religious diversity that does not neglect either the positive or negative aspects of religion. A good example of how to deal with religious diversity has been given by a European project on School and Community that produced ideas for school, classroom and community regarding religion by teachers, pupils and people of faith in different big European cities. The report about this project says:

> It is impossible to prepare pupils to be active partners in creating the new multicultural or intercultural European reality without helping them to appreciate the place and influence of the different religions which are now practised in Europe and in the wider world. For part of being a European is to have a relationship with the rest of the world. We do not wish to replace a narrow nationalism with a narrow "Europeanism". And so we are convinced that pupils can come to learn about and from the great world religions in ways which will give them the skills and attitudes required to live and develop a multi-faith Europe of the future. Racism and xenophobia will not disappear unless children are helped to appreciate that the great religions teach common values and can all be used to fight intolerance and injustice. (Regarding Religion: Ideas for School and Community, published by Bradford Education 1998, p. 8.)

The focus on the common values of the great religions can also help to develop a critical view of any misuse of religion faced today in fundamentalist movements or by political parties that instrumentalise religion for their own purpose.

Four conditions and four approaches

With such a background, the first part (A) of this section considers the following educational conditions for dealing with religious diversity in intercultural education:

- co-operative learning;
- a safe space to foster self-expression;
- use of "distancing" and "simulation";
- empathetic communication.

These conditions are of crucial importance for an intercultural education that takes account of religious diversity. Some deal with individual concepts (such as empathy and distancing) that can be incorporated into various teaching processes in order to help young people understand each other in a better way. Others refer more to a collective and group-oriented learning process (for example co-operative learning and creating a "safe space") and offer insights that are especially suitable for the exploration of inter-religious and intercultural issues.

The second part (B) of this section presents four useful teaching and learning approaches that provide different ways of enabling young people to develop a genuine understanding of others, and that might encourage others to reflect on their own practice:

- the phenomenological approach;
- the interpretive approach;
- the dialogical approach;
- the contextual approach.

A short introduction to each approach is followed by examples from the classroom or wider educational context that should help readers to consider the aims, objectives, skills, competences, methods and outcomes of each approach, and how they might use the approaches in their own context.

A. Educational conditions

1. Co-operative learning

Micheline Milot

Introduction

Promoting tolerance, acceptance of others and reciprocity depends crucially on the kind of educational approach used. Various educational approaches have been devised in recent years depending on many different school contexts (from a social, religious, moral and ethnic point of view). Co-operative learning is one of the basic principles which needs interaction between students through group work to achieve a common goal. Co-operative learning nurtures both academic and social skills. It is distinct from competitive learning, which reduces the chances of success of children who are made to feel inferior because they are less able in certain areas or because they belong to a minority religious or ethnic group.

Co-operative learning helps pupils to learn by placing them in a relational situation enabling them to achieve more easily objectives fitting in with their interests and academic needs through communication and problem resolution. The educational principles inherent in this approach have several advantages which make them particularly appropriate in school contexts where intercultural education incorporates a religious dimension. It encourages critical thinking, tolerance and recognition of diversity. Through the dynamic process created, pupils learn to get to know each other and respect individual differences. We shall look at some of these principles: group/class diversity, positive interdependence, accountability*, reflexivity and equal-status interaction.

1. Group diversity

Diversity (or heterogeneity) within groups of pupils is a key component of co-operative learning, since working together with individuals from different backgrounds is all part of learning to live in society. Researchers maintain that students can learn more easily, from both a social and an academic point of view, when they are in heterogeneous groups. Learning activities should place an emphasis on work in small groups. In particular, care should be taken to ensure that the groups are mixed; this will give rise to mutually enriched discussions and encourage exchanges which will make the participants more open to each other (Cohen 1994, 2002). There are various methods for applying co-operative learning, but they all involve working in small, mixed groups and this is all the more essential when children from different religious or moral backgrounds are learning together in a classroom and have to address issues relating to the diversity of beliefs or moral values.

Diversity relates to academic skills, linguistic skills and background, culture or religion. Teachers should assign learning tasks in such a way as to maximise each pupil's skills or strengths, while at the same time taking account of the level of leadership of each member of the class (Howden and Kopiec 2002; Cohen 1994). So it is not merely a question of grouping young people together to "represent" diversity in the classroom, but of allowing all pupils to play a role within the group in line with their respective skills. Enabling a pupil's specific contribution to be recognised will mean that he or she can develop a sense of success and self-esteem and feel part of the school community. The aim of this interaction within the group is therefore to bring about a sense of positive interdependence among pupils.

2. Positive interdependence

Positive interdependence is reflected in peer empathy (Howden and Kopiec 2002, p. 13) in pursuit of a common goal (which may be, for example, preparations for a religious or secular festival). Positive interdependence is without a doubt the most important component of co-operative learning. It is based on the premise that no-one can accomplish a task alone, and that it requires everyone to pull together in order to achieve a common goal. In other words, "if there is no positive interdependence, there is no co-operation" (Johnson, Johnson and Holubec 1998, p. 1: 13). Positive interdependence can be regarded both as a structure to ensure that pupils work together and as an attitude prevailing in classes, where pupils are concerned not only about their own education but also that of their classmates (Abrami et al. 1996, p. 74).

This approach places an emphasis on learning through application of the values of co-operation: autonomy, participation, respect and communication. It also encourages mutual support, readiness to listen to peers and mutual teaching. Of course, interaction does give scope for potential conflict. Particularly in the field of values and beliefs, diversity does not spontaneously give rise to understanding and tolerance. In this method, students must learn to address controversy and allow an exchange of opinions to take place as this is a fundamental aspect of developing social skills and a positive attitude to diversity.

Mutual support is a key component of co-operative learning and encourages pupils to become involved. It enables pupils to make full use of their social skills, particularly as each member of the group needs to share leadership responsibilities. Such an educational environment is particularly suited to intercultural education which seeks to develop an understanding of diversity and the necessary social skills to live peacefully in a pluralist context.

With the encouragement of the teacher, this interdependence can help pupils develop a positive perception of each individual member of the group. This will be reflected in an attitude of co-operation which, once internalised, will become a genuine value in pupils' eyes (Abrami *et al.* 1996, p. 74). In our opinion, this value lies behind the principles set out in the section on the religious dimension of intercultural education, especially with regard to learning to acknowledge that there are different ways of seeing life, relating to others and working together in pursuit of the common good.

Before moving onto learning activities proper, such an approach should focus on encouraging pro-social behaviour and building up an environment of trust and acceptance of others (Howden and Kopiec 2002, p. 12). These features of co-operative learning should be of particular value to teachers wishing to introduce the religious dimension into intercultural education, where it is not merely a question of passing on knowledge but enabling young people to develop certain skills and attitudes. This approach therefore helps nurture within a social group (a class or school) a sense of individual accountability.*

3. Accountability

Learning implies fostering individual and group accountability, and an emphasis on applying social skills (Totten *et al.* 1991). Such empowerment enables pupils to realise that their contributions are important, that they can become a resource for others and are essential for the success of the group (Cohen 2002). Since the exercise comprises a common goal for the group and a role assigned to each member, this creates a feeling of personal accountability to the group. The religious dimension is not merely a public matter, since individuals often derive their values and motivation to act from a religious or spiritual tradition. In the learning process, it is important to foster capacity for accountability, so essential in peaceful collaboration in a pluralist society. Attitudes of respect, tolerance and openness to dialogue are based necessarily on the conviction that social peace is everyone's responsibility.

4. Reflexivity

Another key component of co-operative learning is to be found in the process of reflection (or reflexivity) to ensure that pupils are aware of the skills they apply or can apply in working sessions. Regardless of the various types of activity that may encourage such reflection, the aim is always the same: critical feedback on conduct and its individual and group effects. It is therefore important to make provision for the time required for this critical examination. This exercise encourages reflection on the values held by each member (equality, equity, respect, justice, honesty, etc.). In addressing the religious dimension of intercultural education, reflection should be introduced as a process in order to help young people adopt a position in a thoughtful, autonomous and responsible way in the light of their own values and the diversity of values. Pupils not only become aware of the diversity of points of view, but are also led to develop aptitudes which will enable them to recognise this plurality and treat it with respect. This process will not only help correct false logic (or prejudice) among pupils, but will also nurture an ability to discuss and reflect (Cohen 1994; Cohen et al. 1994; Johnson, Johnson and Holubec 1998). It enhances the quality of reasoning by generating new ideas and new solutions to conflicts of values and allows for new data (knowledge, values, and attitudes) to be incorporated and internalised.

5. Equal-status interaction

Elizabeth Cohen, a renowned expert in co-operative learning, describes a model which warrants particular attention – that of equal-status interaction to ensure that students learn to discuss and reflect, acknowledging others as equals in diversity. Cohen identifies an inevitable problem for those who wish to implement co-operative learning: inequality between the members of a team. She attributes inequality situations in the classroom to problems of status: a pupil's social status is based, for example, on the family's religious background (especially in the case of children from minority groups), ethnic origin or socio-economic class. She also identifies school status on the basis of the pupils' "academic strength", status among peers, popularity, personality or leadership potential. In the light of these factors of "stigmatisation", teachers and pupils have (often implicit) expectations regarding the skills that each individual should display. The level of these expectations will vary in line with the status implicitly assigned to each child. Cohen maintains that it is not primarily inequality of status that leads to prejudice in the classroom, but rather the expectations of competence assigned to that status (Cohen 2002, 1997a, 1997b). In order to overcome this difficulty, Cohen introduces the concept of the "equitable classroom" (Cohen 2002) which can be brought about in application of two principles: 1) encouraging interaction by making the groups accountable; 2) changing expectations of ability in order to create equal-status interactions (Cohen 2002, p. 162). The teacher should take the appropriate action to "equalise" these statuses as much as possible.

> "Status treatment" is the action designed to create interaction in which statuses are equal (Cohen 2002, p. 154).

Account is taken of the fact that there are multiple skills among the children. Addressing multiple skills means ensuring that pupils take on board the fact that they do not on their own have all the necessary skills to complete a task and that each pupil has certain skills which he or she must maximise for the success of the group and for his or her own and each other's learning. This makes it possible to assign roles which will highlight these skills in such a way as to enhance the pupil's status in the eyes of his or her peers. Consequently, "low-status" pupils will be more confident, participate more and generally perform better because their status will have changed and will no longer be regarded as stigmatisation.

In this way, the pupils' social identity is positively affected by co-operative learning. In a group made up of members of different religious and cultural backgrounds, for example, it is the personal skills and knowledge of the members of the group that become integration criteria rather than their ethnic or religious affiliation. Accordingly, a common identity created by a group identity can be developed through the pursuit of common goals, fostering integration into social units transcending specific affiliations (Gaudet et al. 1998, p. 13). This identity will unite individuals where normally they would be divided: in order to accept diversity, one has to become capable of viewing members of other social categories as members of the same society in which everyone lives together. This is why co-operative learning has a positive effect on acceptance of religious and ethnic differences and on reducing prejudice vis-à-vis different cultures (Totten et al. 1991).

Conclusion

The principles of co-operative learning described above can, in our view, assist teachers wishing to introduce the religious dimension into a concept of intercultural education where it is not merely a question of knowledge passed on, but of the skills and attitudes young people need to acquire.

Key points of the co-operative approach

- Co-operative learning is based on the premise that no-one can accomplish a task alone, and that it requires everyone to pull together in order to achieve a common goal.

- Co-operative learning requires positive interdependence, which can be regarded both as a structure to ensure that pupils work together, where pupils are concerned not only about their own education but also that of their classmates.

- Co-operative learning works in small heterogeneous groups. (Diversity relates to academic skills, linguistic skills and background, culture or religion. Teachers should assign learning tasks in such a way as to maximise each pupil's skills or strengths.)

- Co-operative learning allows the personal skills and knowledge of the members of the group to become integration criteria rather than their ethnic or religious affiliation. This identity will unite individuals where normally they would be divided.

---

2. A "safe space" to foster self-expression

Peter Schreiner

"Children will always need safe places for learning. They will always need launching pads from which to follow their curiosity into the larger world. And they will always need places to make the transition from their childhood homes to the larger society of peers and adults" (Senge 2000, p. 5).

1. Why we need a "safe space" in intercultural education

Schools depend on the communities of which they are part. Their overall mission is to provide knowledge and skills to enable pupils to connect new knowledge to the inner scaffolding they already have, based on their individual and social awareness, experiences, emotions, will, aptitudes, beliefs, values, etc. This includes the orientation for one's own life and also for the communities and the society one lives in. Migration movements in many parts of Europe have created neighbourhoods of people with different cultural backgrounds, religions and ways of living. Plurality is a common feature in Europe's societies. This has especially affected public schools which pupils attend, irrespective of their cultural or religious background. In societies with an increasing plurality of cultures, religions and life-stances, a major issue is how to deal with differences and how to handle conflicts that may arise out of differences. How should we recognise and value cultural differences and, at the same time, promote cultural integration and integral developments of pupils, first at school and also in society? Two objectives of educational activities in school are to provide support for identity formation and to foster mutual understanding. This necessitates a clear recognition of the cultural and religious background of the pupils and students in school because this is an important part of an identity for both minorities and for the majority in a society.

Intercultural education is based on principles that promote openness to the other, respect for difference, mutual understanding, active tolerance, validating the existing cultures, providing equal opportunities and fighting discrimination. These principles are agreed in theory but how to implement them in pedagogical approaches and methods is a challenge. It is no surprise that living together with "the Other" is a difficult task. As human beings we are not well prepared to love and appreciate those who are different from us except members of our family or of the close community to which we belong. In social science we speak of "in-group amity" and "out-group enmity" as two codes of morals. In daily interaction, we make a subtle distinction between "us" and the "others", often on the basis of easily learned binary classifications such as friend/foe or kin/non-kin. Emotions seem to reinforce cognitive discriminations while rational arguments justify or even sanctify our emotional reactions. Conflicting individual interests influence group life and may create social tensions. Co-operation and competition are two sides of communal life in social groups. Conflict theories have taught us that there is a need to create a space and atmosphere of safety and security if a constructive dialogue is to take place between those who are different from each other. It is no surprise that religion can become a difficult dimension of "the Other". Religion is linked to truth claims and truth claims of one religion can differ from truth claims of another religion. But there are also common features of the different religions. They all include perspectives about the meaning of life, about how life is organised, about rituals, dogmas and experiences. These two sides of religion should be equally recognised.

It is with this background that the principle of a "safe space" is vital, in order to allow a constructive dealing with differences. Organising a "safe space" can allow a school to:

- provide a secure environment to foster self-expression;
- explore differences outside a context of insecurity, fear and tension;
- share, tell and listen without ready-made statements;
- foster dialogue-oriented ways of learning;
- begin a process of reconciliation free from hatred and violence.

The concept of "safe space" is a guiding principle for intercultural activities in the classroom. It can create an atmosphere where differences can be expressed without hurting "the Other". It means to provide space for equal participation, to foster self-expression, for sharing stories and for mediating conflicts. It needs an agreement about common rules for dialogue and exchange. It can also be enriched by non-verbal activities and phases of silence. This is not an independent principle but it supports empathetic communication and co-operative learning.

2. How to create a "safe space" – a story of success in Northern Ireland

Integrated schools in Northern Ireland can be seen as a story of success where creating a safe space has been successfully done. The establishment of integrated schools has contributed to reconciliation in the segregated society of Northern Ireland.[4]

2.1. The context

Northern Ireland is a province of the United Kingdom and displays in classic form many of the characteristics of an ethnic frontier community. In Northern Ireland conflict occurs between those who identify with the Irish Republican tradition and those who identify with the British Unionist tradition. This split is reinforced by religion, Republicanism being Catholic, Unionism being Protestant. When the political entity in Northern Ireland was created in 1921, education with the agreement of both communities was divided on sectarian lines. For much of the history of the state, education reflected the political, social, economic, religious and cultural apartheid which characterised this ethnic frontier community. Of the 1,290 schools, 773 are 100% one tradition, that is, controlled (Protestant) or maintained (Catholic) and only 34 have 10% or more of the other tradition. Fifty-seven integrated schools are balanced between the two communities. The effect of this is that many people grow up in Northern Ireland without ever having met someone from the other community. In this way difference is perpetuated and opportunities to challenge stereotypes and prejudice are limited. Integrated schools in Northern Ireland emerged as a number of parents recognised that existing educational systems perpetuated division and that alternatives needed to be offered which would enable young people to meet on a daily basis and work together across previously mutually exclusive traditions. In 1981 the first integrated school, Lagan College, opened in Belfast. In 1985 three more schools opened and by end of 2004 there were 57 integrated schools in Northern Ireland. Integrated education brings together in roughly equal numbers pupils from Protestant and Catholic backgrounds along with pupils from other cultures. A similar balance is aspired to by the staff and Board of Governors of these schools. Integrated schools are inclusive. They are co-educational, all-ability and welcome pupils from all political, religious and socio-economic backgrounds.

2.2. A case study: Brownlow Integrated College

The school was established in 1973 as a controlled (Protestant) school for 11-16-year-old pupils in the new town of Craigavon. Craigavon experienced many acts of violence during the troubles and the communities in

---

4. More information through www.nicie.org.

some parts of the borough are highly polarised. The school "transformed" to become a controlled integrated school in 1991. Brownlow attracts pupils from the greater Craigavon area and has a balance between the two main communities of pupils and on the Board of Governors. Staffing has made significant strides towards balance. The school's motto is "Equality in Community", emphasising the importance of good education in the context of team work and co-operation both among the staff and collaboration with the wider community. The school aspires to "Take the 'fear' out of difference". Brownlow seeks to implement its vision by:

- being a model of an effective, functional plural community;
- examining the curriculum on offer to ensure that all cultures within the school are recognised within the taught programme;
- being a place of inclusion, child-focused and with parental involvement;
- creating forums in which staff can discuss and anticipate contentious issues, for example the Integration in Practice Group;
- developing means by which pupils can practise the principle of integration, for example peer mediation;
- forging links with the wider community and the school, for example the Intergeneration Project;
- acknowledging the power of the hidden curriculum in learning and ensuring the implicit messages are consistent with the ideals of integration.

Brownlow Integrated College is a location where many people can communicate across barriers of religion, culture, traditions and fear. It is a place where people are taken out of the "comfort zone" of mono-culturalism. It has become a place where pupils can learn to "dance with difference" and be enriched, not threatened, by the culture of others.

Key points of a safe space to foster self-expression

A safe space:
- provides a welcoming atmosphere to explore different views in the classroom;
- creates a setting without insecurity, fear and tension;
- provides space for equal participation;
- requires rules of dialogue to allow respect for each other;
- can help organise learning in the classroom.

3. Use of "distancing" and "simulation"

John Keast

Introduction

In the UK, as in many other European countries, intercultural education often takes place through the religious education (RE) curriculum. RE raises questions about the nature and role of religion generally depending on how it is approached. For example, it can be comparative, phenomenological, interpretive, open, pluralistic, critical, allowing for varying degrees of personal involvement and judgement. Recent developments in the UK have seen a high degree of agreement around the two types of pupils' learning that RE should attempt to produce. These are learning about religion and learning from religion. These are specified in the new National Framework for RE[5] published for use in England's schools in 2004, and are also the two attainment targets by which pupils' assessment is measured.

1. Types of learning

Learning about religion "includes enquiry into … the nature of religion, its beliefs, teachings and ways of life, sources, practices and form of expression. It includes skills of interpretation, analysis and explanation" (National Framework for Religious Education, p. 11). It is generally regarded as less contentious and difficult than learning from religion. This is because the subject matter is derived from the relatively objective, though complex, study of the nature of religion in general and religions in particular. Although this type of learning does involve many skills, they are cognitive ones to do with gaining knowledge and understanding of the nature of religion in human life and society, and of the beliefs, expression, practices and impacts of specific religions. Learning from religion "is concerned with developing pupils' reflection on and response to their own and others' experiences in the light of their learning about religion. It develops pupils' skills of application, interpretation and evaluation of what they learn about religion" (National Framework for Religious Education, p. 11). It is regarded as more problematic because it is harder to conceptualise what such

_____
5. Found on www.qca.org.uk/subjects/re.

learning looks like, how it occurs, and how well it is achieved. Learning from religion is more about the individual and his or her community, and less about the subject matter of religion or religions. Learning from religion is about the relevance of religion to the pupil, and the development of various skills of making sense of the knowledge and understanding of religion gained in learning about it. Questions raised in this form of learning might include, "What does the pupil learn about him or herself from learning about religion?" or "What does the pupil learn about his or her family, community or society from learning about religion?"

2. Diversity and dialogue

Both these types of learning in RE are involved in issues of diversity and dialogue. There can be little real learning from religion about oneself, one's own community and those of others without learning about religion; if so, the learning would be based on little knowledge and understanding. Similarly, learning about religion is insufficient in itself to produce the kind of respectful attitudes that community and social cohesion requires in a multi-faith society. Empathy and evaluation, defined by the Archbishop of Canterbury[6] as "taking seriously the seriousness of others and testing it against what one holds seriously oneself" can only happen if what one is learning about others is applied to life and the community. Valuing diversity in European societies, learning to live with and enjoy difference, communicating with and dialoguing with others has to have a substantial basis of knowledge and understanding, but only happens when that knowledge and understanding are employed in raising questions on its relevance and importance.

3. The need for "distancing"

The nature of learning, particularly learning from religion, is not the only sensitive aspect of religious education. For many adults and children, religion is very personal and individual, whether they think religion has a public role or not. For them, religion concerns their private belief and practice. Talking about this in RE can cause some embarrassment, confusion or hesitation, for they may fear being forced to make some confession of their own views or reveal uncertainty or ignorance. They may feel "put on the spot". Sensitivity may be felt by some groups or religious communities, who may fear their views and practices come to be seen as embarrassingly exotic, and who may become defensive as a result. There are also issues of

6. Unpublished speech to the Religious Education Council, London, 4 May 2005.

difference within and between religious communities, and contextual issues or tensions within and between them, either inside or outside school, or both.

It is for all these reasons, and against this background, that methodologies have been developed that promote "distancing" in learning. Ways are needed that allow pupils to engage safely in the kinds of learning described above that do not cause them undue embarrassment, anxiety or distress. Methods are needed to raise and engage pupils in important issues of religious diversity and dialogue that avoid these problems. "Distancing" and "simulation" are two such methods. Their forms of learning are "second hand" and indirect, though no less powerful or effective for being so. They are sufficiently "removed" from the child and his or her own personal life, or from the actual community the child is from, so that they allow study and learning to take place in a safe way, but at the same time they are close enough to the child and community to be realistic, meaningful and relevant to both the aims of study and the child's own capacity to understand and learn.

4. Examples of distancing techniques

These exist in both more and less developed ways. They include:

- the use of real people who represent faiths, beliefs or practices far removed from children in the classroom, such as well-known religious leaders, either local or national. This might be done through forums, video or the internet to give information on and access to how others believe, practise and apply their own religion to life;

- the use of imagined characters in a video or textbook. This is particularly effective if such characters are of the same age as the pupils in the religious education class, such as young people called Zoe, David, Maria, Bilal, etc. to represent various religions' beliefs and practices, which can be studied and evaluated by pupils in the classroom at second hand;[7]

- the use of story and artefacts, internet sites and displays, which produce material at a distance from the pupils in the actual classroom, and to which those pupils can relate personally to a degree of their own choosing.

These techniques are much better than picking on actual children present in the class to represent a religious viewpoint which they may or may not

7. One example is Framework RE, Book 1, Hodder Headline, 2005.

have, depending on the variation of tradition to which they belong, or which they may nor may not be willing to share with others, including the teacher, or by which they may or may not be embarrassed or upset, or fear giving cause for offence to others, whether of their own tradition or a different one.

4.1. A "Gift to the Child"

One very developed form of distancing technique developed by Michael Grimmitt, Julie Grove, John Hull and Louise Spencer at the University of Birmingham in 1996 was entitled "A Gift to the Child". This was a teaching and learning strategy for young children based on a number of pieces of content. An example, based on the call to prayer, used four stages and two devices, one of which was Distancing. After engaging with the content or topic of study, the pupils discovered more about it, such as to whom it belonged. The call to prayer was engaged by the children hearing it, and then they entered into it further to discover more about it and discovered that it belonged to Yaseen, a small Muslim boy. In order to contextualise this and enable the young pupils to go on to reflect on its importance, a distancing device is used. The purpose of this is to set up:

> a boundary which most children may not cross ... This enables the teacher and children to speak about the religious material in the third person. This may not be what you do ... No assumptions are made about faith; children learn to respect each other's faiths and to accept differences. At the same time the identity of the child from the religious tradition being studied can be strengthened. Children who come from no particular religious family background will still enjoy the richness of the images ...[8]

The deliberate use of a distancing device removes the topic of study from being too close to any one child in the class to a kind of representative child who may be referred to safely by all the children and the teacher. After the technique has been used, the content being studied can be contextualised and reflected upon in a safe way, applicable to all pupils. A number of examples of this technique have been developed and resourced by a useful book for teachers and picture books for young children, on topics such as Our Lady of Lourdes, Ganesha, Angels, Jonah and Nanak's song.

5. Simulations and examples

Simulations are another useful technique. Here the distancing device is more complex and structured into a real life situation that is some distance

---

8. Grimmitt, M., *A Gift to the Child*, Simon and Schuster Education, 1991, ISBN 0 7501 0128 8.

from the actual pupils' situation but is one to which they can relate. Religious and moral dilemmas that are not necessarily theirs can be created for pupils to engage with in the religious education classroom, but might be close enough to them for them to develop points of understanding. Examples may include:

- case studies of a religious or moral dilemma, such as Sabbath observance (opening of shops on Sundays), medical ethics (assisted suicide), conflict of interests in friendship (when to keep a promise) and truth claims (who is right about creation?);

- simulated situations that specifically focus on questions of diversity and dialogue. One example is an imaginary meal, where three famous religious figures of the past are invited to share the same table at dinner. Pupils draw a diagram of a round table and three chairs with the names of the figures on them. In between the chairs, pupils identify and record what each of the two religious leaders sitting next to each other have in common. On the table they identify and list the issues on which they seem to have no agreement – issues that are still "on the table" for resolution. These can then be discussed "at a distance" from the pupils' own situations yet reflect the situations of diversity in which they really live.

6. Resources

The methodologies described above require appropriate resources. The most important of these is the right ethos and learning climate. There has to be a safe environment for this kind of study. Part of the resource, then, is a set of rules, agreed with and by the pupils themselves for the kind of learning that is to take place. These rules might include not just things like not calling out, not being disrespectful, but always saying something positive. Similarly, a skilled teacher is required, for without sufficient training teachers would not only not think of these techniques but not be experienced in using them. Teachers need also to have clear objectives for this kind of teaching and learning so that they know what it is that they want the pupils to achieve, and how they might best achieve it. An important part of such training is the use of the imagination by teachers so that they can create the right kind of distancing techniques and simulation situations, and stimulate the pupil's imaginations to enter into them. Sources of information are needed especially if the pupils are to work at a distance from themselves. These might include relevant, accurate and accessible texts, but also a range of artefacts.

Key points of use of distancing and simulation

- Both learning about and learning from religion are necessary if the religious dimension of intercultural education is to be taken seriously.

- Distancing techniques allow pupils to engage in intercultural and inter-religious dialogue in a safe way, without embarrassment or fear.

- Distancing techniques include the use of third parties, imaginary figures, artefacts, and other forms of "indirect" teaching and learning.

- Simulations represent complex situations where learning is achieved through the resolution of dilemmas or imaginative use of other constructions to identify and discuss issues.

4. Empathetic communication

Albert Raasch

Introduction

Empathy is a key concept. It helps us in three respects:

- to gain a better knowledge of others;
- to gain a better understanding of ourselves;
- to improve our relationships with others.

Empathy can therefore help to trigger discovery, increase understanding and develop social cohesion. There are many aspects to this concept. Empathy is a dynamic mental and emotional stimulus, not a state of mind. It relates to individuals as well as communities, and to interrelations between individuals and community. Empathy can therefore make a key contribution to resolving intercultural problems, particularly regarding religious diversity. It is particularly applicable to education, educational theory and school teaching, offering a whole range of methodological approaches to learning, concerned with reflection, emotiveness and participation.

This account of empathy is organised as follows:

- Part 1: horizontal and vertical dimensions of empathy, and current definitions.
- Part 2: application of linguistic findings with reflections on individual concepts of empathy.
- Part 3: application of these to achieve a better understanding of oneself and others.
- Part 4: situations that can create, encourage, hinder or prevent empathy: the inter-human dimension.

Clearly these reflections do not lead to momentary or short-lived results but constitute a continuous process in which results may develop, change, and be modified, disappear or be replaced by others. The presentation therefore follows a plan that reflects this dynamism and has been shown to be effective in another Council of Europe project entitled European

Language Portfolio.[9] As an educational tool, the Portfolio takes various forms to take account of its different target groups. The presentation in this reference book is simply one of a number of variants. An assessment of definitions of "empathy" (Part 1) is followed by the three parts concerned with learners' mental structure, self-assessment and action plans. The Portfolio therefore touches on the three basic dimensions of cognition, affection and behaviour, or knowledge, self-awareness and know-how. This Portfolio is relevant to interculturalism in general and the religious and interfaith dimension in particular.

1. Empathy

A number of definitions are used in current discussions. Two approaches emerge:

- a psychological approach; and
- a linguistic approach.

These offer a basis for reflection, or a sort of springboard for greater understanding of empathy. On the basis of Part 1, Part 2 offers an opportunity to choose or create your personal and subjective concept of empathy, that is, start off with what others have come up with and then find your own way forward.

A. From a psychological standpoint, empathy is a skill, that of putting yourself in the place of others. In this sense, empathy can therefore be learnt. I can develop a strategy or technique to assemble, in the ideal case, a maximum of data on others, on their mental apparatus, the context in which they live, their past experience, their intentions and aspirations, their state of mind and so on. Drawing on this data I can understand their actions, past and present, or predict how they will behave in the future. Empathy is therefore the art of putting me in the place of others, without necessarily sympathising with them. All the same, the very fact of becoming so involved with another may lead to my not only understanding but also sympathising with him or her. Empathy is therefore not a state but a continually developing process. Different levels of empathy can be attained and it may culminate in other psychological states, such as sympathy. Empathy may derive from the personality of the person who experiences it, for example from a sense of charity. But equally, or alternatively, the other person's situation may trigger empathy. In other words, empathy can signify activity (putting oneself in the place of others) and/or passivity (being subjected to their influence). These two aspects are often

9. http://www.coe.int/T/DG4/Portfolio/.

intermingled, thus highlighting the complexity of the phenomenon. Empathy may lead to a state of psychological constraint. On the other hand, human beings have need of others who offer their empathy because this is essential for the development of identity, particularly in children. Empathy therefore includes a strong social element. In this sense, it is a force for cohesion among members of a society.

B. From a semantic standpoint, empathy may be compared with:

- would-be or quasi-synonyms, such as sympathy, respect, tolerance, charity, love, having a weakness for, having affection for, and interest in;

- would-be or quasi-antonyms, such as indifference, lack of sensitivity, reserve, coldness, antipathy, egotism, insensitivity, impassivity, disinterest and neutrality;

- connotations such as humanist approach, humanitarian approach and altruism;

- vertical semantic structures, such as feeling (hyperonym), or ones that are still higher in the semantic hierarchy, such as mental or psychological dispositions and attitudes (super-hyperonyms);

- verbal constructions that combine with empathy, such as experience, feel, acknowledge, acquire, show evidence of, and lack;

- gradations, such as indifference, empathy, sympathy, friendship, love and passion;

- attributives such as inadequate, growing, great, and excessive;

- terms that indicate changes in empathy, such as develop, grow, decline and fade away;

- terms that indicate reactions, such as criticise, be ashamed of and hide;

- morphosyntactic terms (terms that exist or have emerged) such as empathy, empathetic, empathise (= sympathise) with, empathising (= sympathising); and analogies that show difference and specific circumstances, such as more/less/the most empathetic (= sympathetic); someone/something is empathetic (= sympathetic);

- objective terms and expressions, such as feel empathy for someone or something or someone's attitude, behaviour, reactions and opinions;

- subjective terms and expressions, such as "someone or something inspires empathy in me", or "is a source of empathy to me".

2. Reflections on concepts of empathy

Here we reflect on what we understand by empathy, using a number of analytical questions.

a. How to use the two approaches, psychological and linguistic, to identify, define or localise my feelings:

- What do I feel about a real person, an idea or another person's behaviour and words?

- Do I really feel empathy?

- Is what I feel possibly not so much empathy as sympathy? (See Part 1b: synonyms.)

- What awakens this feeling of empathy/sympathy etc. in me? (See Part 1b: subjective terms.)

- What prevents me from feeling empathy? (See Part 1b: terms that indicate reactions.)

b. How to assess what I feel:

- Is my empathy justified and if so, how?
- Is my empathy developing, and if so, in what direction?

c. How to recognise what my feelings of empathy trigger:

- Do I show general tolerance towards the world: yes/no/sometimes/don't know?

- Do I show empathetic tolerance to specific persons or phenomena (another person's behaviour, clothes, utterances and so on)?

- Do I accept others despite ... (what prevents me from feeling empathy)?

- Do I admire others/difference/diversity?

- Do I regularly check my feelings (of empathy)?

- Do I check my actions/attitudes/behaviour in relation to my feelings?

- Do I assess my feelings by comparing them with experiences/thinking/impressions?

- Am I am unable to feel empathy, even though there is nothing to prevent me from doing so, something I find difficult to explain?

- Do I have to make an effort to feel empathy for someone/something?

3. Applying these reflections

Here we ask certain questions about our attitudes, ideas and behaviour in order to achieve greater self-awareness:

- What are my behaviour, attitudes, intentions and ideas in relation to empathy?
- What consequences do I draw from comparing my thinking on empathy with my actual behaviour?
- Can I draw any conclusions about how to organise my life?

4. Situations to encourage the inter-human dimension

Here we ask what makes us think, feel, act and react as we do, and offer a few suggestions for increasing our understanding of the contexts which influence or control us. What are the forces that spur us on? It is here that intercultural factors come fully into play, and the values and the hierarchy of values become predominant and perhaps, even, inevitable.

- The utterances of others:
  - their words (lexical level): what they mean and any additional connotations;
  - how they are assembled (lexical field, degree of coherence, style);
  - the functions of utterances (pragmatic level, statements, statements in relation to situations and roles).

- External or extra-verbal aspects:
  - physical aspect (face, eyes, etc.);
  - gestures;
  - body language;
  - muscle movements;
  - clothing.

- Others' ideas and concepts (semantic-notional level):
  - thematic content;
  - the intentions behind the choice of theme;
  - what is not said.

- Others' attitude:
  - method of acting and behaving;
  - method of discussing and negotiating;
  - method of co-operating.

- The general impression that others evoke:
  - confidence;
  - competence;
  - truthfulness;
  - experience;
  - creativity;
  - freshness of spirit;
  - (non-)conformity;
  - traditionalism/modernity.

This portfolio is therefore an educational tool that aims to establish that each of us has a responsibility towards others, be it persons, cultures or religions. It is not a final and complete version but a set of proposals that is open to change.

Key points of the empathetic approach

- Empathy is not a state of mind but a dynamic mental and emotional stimulus.

- Empathy helps us to a better knowledge of others, a better understanding of ourselves and to improve our relationships with others.

- Empathy can be approached from psychological and semantic standpoints.

- We can ask many questions of ourselves to assess our level of empathy and improve our empathetic communication.

B. LEARNING APPROACHES

1. The phenomenological approach

Robert Jackson

Introduction

There are a number of variants of the phenomenological approach to the study of religious diversity. These are rooted in the discipline of the phenomenology of religion rather than in sociological phenomenology. Some key elements of the general approach are:

- to teach in order to promote knowledge and understanding, not to promote a particular religious or non-religious view;

- to avoid imposing one's own views and attitudes upon another's religion or way of life;

- as far as it is possible, to empathise with the person from another religion or way of life;

- to distinguish between understanding and judgement or evaluation – the task of phenomenology is to understand, not to evaluate.

Some of these principles are summed up by the French phenomenologist, Gaston Berger:

> The phenomenological method ... teaches us that if we find it impossible to suppress our own beliefs and our own personal feelings when studying human material, we can at least put them into parentheses, so that they become suspended, without our having to become unfaithful to them, and we can sympathize with other people's deepest emotions, without having to approve all acts into which those are translated. The phenomenologist thus stops confusing truth and meaning. He does not necessarily regard everything he describes as true or good, but through various examples, he applies himself to the task of discovering deep-lying structures, the meaning of which becomes clear to him. He is like a faithful translator who is prepared to respect the thought of his author, even when he is aware that he does not approve him. Later, perhaps, he will be his judge, but for the time being, he only wants to be his friend (Berger 1957; English translation in Waardenburg 1973, p. 665).

An English project associated with the British scholar Ninian Smart described the phenomenological approach as follows:

> [The phenomenological approach] ... uses the tools of scholarship in order to enter into an empathic experience of the faith of individuals and groups. It does not seek to promote any one religious viewpoint ... (Schools Council 1971, p. 21).

Phenomenological approach in religious education

The phenomenological approach to the study of religions tends not to be used in its "pure" theoretical form in syllabuses, curricula, textbooks or in the class-room. However, certain aspects of the approach have influenced ways of thinking about religious education and its didactics. These include its methodological neutrality, the "bracketing" of the truth claims of the religious traditions as well as of the values and judgement of the teacher and the pupils, and the comparison of cross-cultural religious phenomena like myth or ritual.

One variant of the phenomenological approach concentrates on looking at religion thematically. Sacred space, rituals, festivals, ideas of divinity, etc. are compared across different religions. One problem with this is that examples of religion are often taken out of their social or cultural context. Some serious mistakes can be made if religions are not considered in a contextual way. Another problem is that like might not be compared with like. For example, the category "sacred scripture" means something rather different in the Hindu and Muslim traditions.

Another criticism of the phenomenological approach is that it gives a purely descriptive account of the externals of religion, and fails to convey the emotional depth of religious commitment. This criticism is valid in the case of some badly produced textbooks and materials, but is not applicable to the best phenomenological materials or to the phenomenological approach in principle.

Some phenomenologists recommend methods which take account of the above criticisms. For example, the Dutch scholar Jacques Waardenburg regards phenomenology as being especially relevant to the contemporary study of living religions, arguing that "religion" should be studied in the context of other factors, for example, social, cultural and economic aspects of life. The study of examples of living religions is a key feature of the method, as is systematic reflection on the process of study. Moreover, Waardenburg insists that phenomenology should engage with linguistic and conceptual issues, and should not impose categories from one way of life or religion on another (Waardenburg 1978, p. 102). Waardenburg sees the researcher's role in reconstructing the religious world of the insider as close to that of an actor playing a part in a play. If we apply that idea to pedagogy for schools, the use of imagination through the employment of methods such as role play and drama would be encouraged in order to try to reconstruct someone else's religious ideas or feelings. Such an approach would answer those critics who claim that the phenomenological approach only deals with the externals of religion.

If the criticisms mentioned above are taken into account in designing materials and activities, then the phenomenological approach can be a useful way to teach and learn about religions in an impartial way. The approach is especially suitable in situations where pupils and teachers are expected not to share their own personal views on religion.

Illustration 1: "Sagesses et religions du monde"

France

An example of some school materials which take a broadly phenomenological approach, and which take care not to impose the categories from one tradition on to another, is a series of books written and published in France for children (mainly in Catholic schools) in the series *Sagesses et Religions du Monde* (World Religions and Wisdom), which includes the texts *Les Fêtes Religieuses* (Religious Festivals) and *Les Lieux du Sacré* (Sacred Places) (Defebvre and Estivalezes 2003a and b).

Les Lieux du Sacré takes year 4 students through religious symbolism, introducing examples from different religious traditions. The book then moves to places of worship in Jewish, Christian (covering Catholic, Orthodox and Protestant traditions), Muslim, Hindu and Buddhist contexts. The book then considers some key sacred cities, towns and sites – Jerusalem as a sacred place in relation to Judaism, Christianity and Islam, Santiago de Compostela (Saint-Jacques de Compostelle) in relation to Christianity and Borobudur in Java in relation to Buddhism. Finally there is some consideration of sacred space in the domestic situation through the examples of family altars and shrines in African traditional religion and Hindu tradition, and domestic objects in the context of Judaism, Christianity and Islam.

Les Fêtes Religieuses, aimed at year 5 pupils, considers the nature and diversity of festivals in human experience, before moving, in relation to a range of religious traditions, to rites of passage (connected with birth, initiation, marriage and death), holy days and calendrical systems. The book then moves on to consider some of the main festivals from Judaism, Christianity (with Catholic, Orthodox and Protestant examples), Islam, Hinduism, Buddhism and nature ("animistic") religions. In the case of each book, questions related to each double page spread are designed to reinforce knowledge and understanding, to engage children with illustrations or selected text or to encourage appropriate comparison and contrast. Occasionally, through the use of carefully constructed questions, children are asked to relate the material to their own personal views and experiences.

Illustration 2: Knowledge, understanding and tolerance

Tim Jensen, Denmark

Denmark is one country in which the approach has been used for many years in the upper-secondary school (gymnasium), where religious education consists of teaching about the various religious traditions and the various religious phenomena. Elements of the phenomenological approach, as used in university studies of religions, are reflected in official documents, guidelines for teachers and in textbooks. The aims of the teaching are said to be knowledge and understanding, based upon an impartial or neutral approach. Students are encouraged to learn about religion at a distance, from the point of view of outsiders, in which religion is seen as a human and social construct. Using skills of empathy, students are also encouraged to see religion from the point of view of insiders. Via this approach to the study of religions, pupils can learn and accept that religions and religious phenomena can be understood from many perspectives – secular, scientific, religious and more. A recent research project based in Denmark indicates that this kind of religious education is very popular amongst students. The respondents suggest that this approach leads to more knowledge, understanding and tolerance.

Key points of the phenomenological approach

- There is a range of phenomenological approaches to the study of religious diversity. These are rooted in the discipline of the phenomenology of religion rather than in sociological phenomenology. Some key elements of the approach are:

- to teach in order to promote knowledge and understanding, not to promote a particular religious or non-religious view;

- to avoid imposing one's own views and attitudes upon another's religion or way of life;

- as far as it is possible, to empathise with the person from another religion or way of life;

- to distinguish between understanding and judgement – the task of phenomenology is to understand, not to judge.

- One variant of this approach is to look at religion thematically, taking great care only to compare like with like.

- One criticism of the phenomenological approach is its failure to get "inside" a religion.

- However, the approach can allow methods such as role play and drama to try to reconstruct someone else's religious ideas or feelings.

2. The interpretive approach

Robert Jackson

Introduction

The interpretive approach aims to provide methods for developing understanding of different religious traditions that can be used by all children of school age. The interpretive approach has some things in common with the phenomenological approach. For example, it aims to increase knowledge and understanding and it sets out neither to promote nor to undermine religious belief. The interpretive approach takes account of the diversity that exists within religions and allows for the interaction of religion and culture, for change over time and for different views as to what a religion is. It can begin with examples from religious traditions, or it can begin with students' questions and concerns. This does not matter, provided the three key concepts of representation, interpretation and reflexivity are covered.

The interpretive approach was developed at the University of Warwick in England (Jackson 1997, 2004a, b, c, d, 2005a, b, c), and has been used in other countries, such as Germany, Norway and South Africa. Its methodology emerged from the experience of field studies of children and young people from different religious backgrounds in Britain, using the methods of ethnography or social anthropology (for example Jackson and Nesbitt 1993; Nesbitt 2004) together with insights from literature from other fields, such as hermeneutics (theory of interpretation) and cultural theory. It is thus an approach grounded in the social sciences.

1. Key concepts

The interpretive approach employs three key concepts in relation to the analysis of religious diversity, namely representation, interpretation and reflexivity.

1.1. Representation

Using scholarly sources from cultural theory and the history of the portrayal of religion and religions in Western literature, the approach is sceptical of post-Enlightenment ways of representing "world religions" as homogeneous systems of belief (Said 1978; Smith 1978). Religions are pictured flexibly in terms of a relationship between individuals within the context of particular groups and wider religious traditions. The study of individuals, in the context of the various groups with which they are associated, informs an emerging understanding of religious traditions. At the same time, key concepts from the religions are exemplified and enlivened through the consideration of particular examples of religious faith and practice.

The approach is equally critical of simplistic representations of cultures and of the relationship between religion and culture which see religions and cultures as internally homogeneous and clearly distinct from one another. Key debates in social anthropology and other social sciences are utilised in developing more sophisticated models of the representation of cultures, cultural processes and ethnicity (for example Barth 1981; Baumann 1996; Clifford 1988). "Cultures" are seen as dynamic, internally contested and fuzzy edged, while individuals are recognised as capable of contributing to the reshaping of culture through making personal syntheses which might draw from a wide range of cultural resources, including their own ancestral traditions. "Culture" is thus represented as both a possession and a process. The approach thus takes on board both the dimension of "traditional" plurality – the overt diversity to be seen through the presence of different religious and ethnic groups in society – and that of "modern" or "post-modern" plurality, in which individuals from any background can utilise cultural ideas and practices from many possible sources (see Chapter 2 above). The interaction of these two dimensions accounts for some of the ideological and spiritual diversity to be found within religious traditions (Jackson 2004a).

With regard to the representation of religions, the interpretive approach uses three "levels".

a. The broadest level is the "tradition". The term "tradition" or "religious tradition" is preferred to "religion". Thus the Christian tradition encompasses all the different denominational and cultural manifestations of Christianity. Immediately it is clear that it would be impossible to have a full grasp of this. It is also clear that different insiders and outsiders would have different views about the scope of the tradition. This does not matter. Each of us (whether teacher or student) can gradually form our own idea of the traditions and the relationship between them. Every time we learn something new, our previous understanding of the tradition is challenged and might be modified. A discussion and analysis of key concepts fits best into this level, and can help to give a provisional framework for understanding that can be modified as more learning takes place.

b. The next level is that of the "group". This might be a denominational or sectarian group, or it might be an ethnic group, or some combination of these. A project on some work based on a family with an Islamic background or on the local church would be informative about groups; and would also influence and inform our understanding of the wider tradition.

c. The third level is that of the "individual". Every individual is unique. It is at this level that we can appreciate best the human face of religion and hear personal stories that break stereotypes.

The exploration of the relationship between these different "levels" can be liberating. You do not feel that you have to know everything, because every example studied illuminates the wider picture. The approach is very flexible. In terms of pedagogy and didactics, you can start with any of the following:

- an overview of key concepts from a tradition;
- a personal story (whether from a visitor to the school or another source);
- the study of a group of some kind;
- pupils' own previous knowledge and experience (including their own experience of religious practice or the absence of religion from their lives).

If you start with key concepts, then you have to make it clear that you are not giving a definitive account, but are just providing an initial framework for understanding. When you look at some individual examples from real life, the general picture will need to be revised.

1.2. Interpretation

The approach's interpretive methods most closely relate to debates in interpretive anthropology (Geertz 1983; Clifford 1988) and to theory from hermeneutics (Gadamer 1975; Ricoeur 1988). Rather than asking students to leave their presuppositions to one side – as in the phenomenological approach – the method requires a comparison and contrast between the learner's concepts and those of the "insider". The approach employs a movement backwards and forwards between the learner's and the "insider's" concepts and experiences. Sensitivity on the part of the student is very important and a necessary condition for empathy. The other aspect of this hermeneutical approach lies in *applying* the model of representation outlined above – moving to and fro between individuals in the context of their groups and the wider religious tradition. These two elements overlap in practice.

The interpretive methodology was not only influenced by discussions of theory and methodology, but was informed by direct experience of ethnographic fieldwork. Studies of children in Britain from a range of different religious and cultural settings were used as a basis for methodological reflection and as a source of material for curriculum development. Thus the earliest materials produced using the approach presented the ways of life of children and young people, observed and interviewed in the context of their families and communities (for example Jackson 1997, 95-120). Some of the texts were written about young children for young children (Barratt 1994a, b, c, d, e); while others featured adolescents and were aimed at young people in lower secondary schools (Mercier 1996, Robson 1995, Wayne *et al* 1996). In all cases, the children and young people and their families who were featured in the books had a role in the development and editing of the texts and the selection of photographs. Later developments of the approach used other starting points, such as key concepts or pupils' questions (see the illustrations below). The approach is flexible and can start at any point on the hermeneutical circle of learning – examples from religions, key concepts, pupils' experiences and questions.

1.3. Reflexivity

The interpretive approach does not simply set out to increase knowledge. It takes the view that, in order to increase understanding, pupils need to reflect on the impact of their new learning on their previous understanding. The approach also gives the learner an active involvement in the learning process. This reflexive element is very much part of modern social science. For example, anthropologists are trained to reflect on the influence of their own background and previous education on their interpretation of new cultural material. Thus, reflexivity covers various aspects of the relationship between the experience of students and the experience of those whose way of life they are attempting to interpret.

Three elements are especially important for the interpretive approach:

- learners re-assessing their understanding of their own worldview;
- learners making a distanced critique of material studied;
- learners developing a running critique of the interpretive process through the review of methods of study.

Approaches to teaching and learning aim to encourage reflection and constructive criticism and require methods that give a voice to pupils, allowing them to gain insight from their peers and to be able to examine different ideas of truth held within the classroom. The "content" of lessons is thus an interactive relationship between material provided by the teacher and the knowledge and experience of the participants. The approach aims for a conversational form of learning which can accommodate diversity and difference.

Since learning is seen as a hermeneutical process, attention needs to be given to students' reflection on their own worldviews in the light of their studies. Reflexive activity is intimately related to the process of interpretation. Interpretation might start from the insider's language and experience, then move to that of the student, and then shift between the two. Thus the process of understanding another's way of life is inseparable in practice from that of considering the issues and questions raised by it.

The approach helps learners to engage with difference. Whatever differences there might appear to be between the student's worldview and the way of life being studied, there may also be points of contact and overlap as well as common elements. What might appear to be entirely different on first acquaintance can end up linking with the learner's own experience in ways that challenge unquestioned assumptions.

Part of the reflexive process is to be able to engage critically with that which is studied. The management of such critical work is an important pedagogical issue, especially in teaching situations that are strongly pluralistic. Pupils need to learn how to be critical in a sensitive and constructive way. Another role for criticism as an element of reflexivity is pupils' involvement with reviewing study methods. This can reveal issues of representation and can also generate creative ideas for improvement, in the presentation of material studied to others. It can also help students to become more aware of bias in the techniques used in other forms of presentation.

2. Younger children and the interpretive approach

The first experiments with the interpretive approach used specially written texts for young children aged 5-8, based on material (interviews, field notes and photographs) collected during field studies of children and their families. For young children, each pupil's book focuses on a single child from one religious group. Each tells a story illustrating how children learn through participation in religious activities within the family (Barratt 1994a, b, c, d, e). There are two versions of each pupil text, one printed in the

Teacher's Resource Book to be read by the teacher and used as a basis for discussion (Jackson, Barratt and Everington 1994), and a simpler text for pupils reproduced in the children's books. The interpretive process is also introduced in the materials in the Teacher's Resource Book which help children to relate concepts, feelings and attitudes encountered in the stories to their own language and experience. Concepts identified from the pages of the story books are grouped together under general headings as "key ideas". These general concepts suggest areas where bridges can be made from pupils' experience of life to the experience of the children introduced in the story. "Bridging" to and from pupils' concepts, feelings and attitudes and those of the characters in the stories is intended to help children to interpret an unfamiliar way of life. It also raises questions in relation to the pupils' own experience. The approach has been developed subsequently using a variety of starting points.

3. Implementing the interpretive approach

You may find some of these suggestions useful in preparing material for teaching:

- Be aware of your own previous knowledge and assumptions.
- Think about the ways in which you interpret religious people's concepts, values, beliefs, rituals, etc. Do you find yourself making connections (bridges) between your world(s) and the worlds of those you are meeting?
- Notice how you revise your understanding of each tradition as you encounter more examples of its practice.
- Avoid, if you can, generalising about a religious tradition. "Some", "a few" and "many" are useful words to use when teaching about religions. Even more useful is the three-fold structure of individual, group and wider tradition introduced above. One theme that will recur is diversity; and the need to identify strategies that you and your colleagues can use to prevent stereotyping.
- Identify ways in which you can implement the three-fold structure (representation, interpretation, reflexivity) to help you organise material about each tradition effectively.
- Building a vocabulary/concepts list for each tradition will be helpful.
- Contacting friends and colleagues who belong to the faith communities you are studying may build your confidence further.
- Question all your sources to find out where the authors/speakers are themselves "coming from".

- You can start with material from a religious tradition, or with pupils' questions and interests. It does not matter so long as the principles of representation, interpretation and reflexivity are covered during the project.

Key points of the interpretive approach

- Religious traditions should be presented, not as homogeneous and bounded systems, but in ways that recognise diversity within religions and the uniqueness of each member, as well as the fact that each person is subject to many influences

- Students should not be expected to set aside their own presuppositions (as in phenomenology), but should compare their own concepts with those of others: "the students' own perspective is an essential part of the learning process".

- Students should re-assess their own ways of life; they should be constructively critical of the material they study; and they should maintain an awareness of the methods they are using, reflecting on the nature of their learning. These three are elements of reflexivity.

3.1. Illustration 1: Learning about the "other" using the interpretive approach

Kevin O'Grady, United Kingdom

Introduction

This example shows a development of the interpretive approach through the use of action research in a school. One of my teaching groups worked together with me to plan and assess a topic of religious education whilst I simultaneously gathered data on factors in their motivation to learn. The topic could equally have been taught as part of citizenship education.

Topic and method

The topic concerned was about Islam. The school had almost no Muslim students despite its location in a large, culturally diverse city, and 12 to 13-year-old students had no real prior knowledge of Islam. Before the teaching started they added their own questions to the school scheme of work; they also wrote down their preferences for styles of learning. The first few lessons were planned accordingly, and at two further points in the topic this consultation was repeated, students additionally reflecting back on what they had learned from the lessons. I kept my own log of observations throughout. Towards the end of the project the students were interviewed about the process as a whole. There was evidence that involving students as collaborative researchers and planners of work had increased their motivation:

- "It definitely motivates you, if you're looking forward to something, because you've planned it yourself."
- "It makes you feel in control, if you're planning the lesson. I don't think you should plan the whole lesson, but you should have a say in it."

The key concepts of the interpretive approach were used as follows:

- With regard to representation, students became aware that stereotypes of Islam, as found commonly in the media, for example, did not match the diversity of the religious lives of real people.
- With regard to interpretation, students learned how to compare and contrast Islamic concepts with ideas from their own experience, and explored some of these similarities and differences through drama.
- With regard to reflexivity, students were prompted to reflect on their own values and cultural assumptions by bringing their own questions and ideas into a dialogue with the Islamic material; this generated real intercultural understanding. It was not face-to-face dialogue, but it was

still a dialogue with difference that built self-awareness and cultural understanding, as the following example shows.

Example

In a lesson about family life, the students formed drama groups and most groups prepared sketches about what they believed to be important in family life. There was a separate group who researched Islamic beliefs about family life from a variety of texts and noted five key factors on a poster for display. We saw and discussed each sketch, making points of contact with the research poster. There was a discussion about extended families: there were traditional working class patterns of extended families in the local area, and the students value care for the elderly. This proved a good way to deconstruct some of their earlier assertions about Muslims "sticking together in large groups in one area". Muslims became less exotic, through the experience of cultural comparison.

Several interview responses illustrated the students' experience of increased self-understanding through the interpretation of Islam:

- "The link is because, when we learn about different religions, you find out who you are ... whether you're Christian, or some people don't want to be different things ... you find out who you are inside."

- "We learn about Muslim life, then about whether it relates to us, in our life."

- "In Islam, they have set rules, like you should always help your elders, and it's made people think that we should always help our parents, too."

Another key element of reflexivity is the importance given to the students' own voices at the centre of enquiry.

Possibilities for wider application

The question arises, how can religious diversity be studied – using the interpretive approach – in subjects other than religious education? The example above of learning about Islam and family life could be modified to fit the context of a social studies or citizenship topic on the family. I have often used an interpretive pedagogy in citizenship teaching, for example in work on beliefs and values in contemporary society where one can begin with an examination of students' own attitudes and comparisons can then be made to those of others. Whatever the area of curriculum, the point is to put students into a hermeneutical relationship with source material. In this way their own values become objects of reflection and they are enabled to reflect on their shifts in awareness.

3.2. Illustration 2: Using the interpretive approach to motivate pupils aged 11-12

Amy Whittall, United Kingdom

Introduction

This example deals with the interpretive approach, but also makes use of empathy skills, dialogue and elements of co-operative learning. The task was to design and teach an approach to the study of religious diversity that would help to motivate pupils who had felt there was little challenge in their studies. The aim was to produce well-informed students, but also to engage them with the material studied so that they had opportunities to consider their personal response to key questions. The project also aimed to help pupils to evaluate their own and others' responses and as a result to reflect on their initial ideas. Use was also made of the following pedagogical principles and pedagogical strategies (through which principles are put into practice) to develop appropriate classroom methods.

1. Generic Pedagogical Principle: challenge, thinking skills, flexible learning:

• Challenge must be an integral part of all lessons.

• In order to challenge pupils, lessons should involve cognitive thinking skills such as problem solving and investigation.

• All learning should be flexible. Pupils should approach information openly and be allowed opportunities to empathise with the material. Lessons should give pupils opportunities to think and make decisions about the knowledge they gain and to transfer information between different areas of the subject.

2. Religious Education Pedagogical Principle 1:

• The study of religions should wherever possible encompass the key principles of the interpretive approach, concerning representation, interpretation and reflexivity.

3. Religious Education Pedagogical Principle 2:

• Pupils should be challenged in their work in order that they can aim to achieve at the highest levels in terms of knowledge, understanding and reflection.

4. Pedagogical strategies

In order to make the project challenging for pupils, the following strategies were employed, all related to the pedagogical principles outlined above. Pupils should be:

- able to move backwards and forwards between the "parts" of a tradition (for example what an individual believes) and the broad context of the tradition;
- encouraged to raise and address individual questions and areas of interest;
- provided with opportunities to pose a question and develop a hypothesis about the answer using previous knowledge and understanding;
- encouraged to decide upon the methods to be used to investigate their hypotheses;
- given opportunities to develop a dialogue between themselves, their peers and members of the tradition in order to investigate their hypothesis;
- encouraged to compare and contrast concepts from the religious tradition with their own nearest equivalent concepts;
- given the opportunity to reflect upon their discoveries both in terms of their knowledge of the tradition and their own ideas and values.

Classroom application: introducing Buddhism

The principles and strategies outlined above were developed into a topic on Buddhism for a class of 11 and 12 year-olds. All activities dealt with at least one of the key elements from the interpretive approach (representation, interpretation, reflexivity).

The pupils had previously done very little on Buddhism and therefore had to move constantly between the small picture of Buddhism they had and the emerging picture they discovered (Strategy 1). As there was little prior knowledge, pupils were encouraged to raise questions they had about Buddhism (Strategy 2). Pupils were given time to discuss in groups the questions they had written individually and explain why these were of interest to them. The groups focused on the two questions they would like to address and these became their focus. It was important to allow pupils to develop a hypothesis using previous knowledge (Strategy 3). To enable the pupils to do this, they were asked to record their initial answers to the two questions drawing on any previous knowledge. This became their hypothesis.

Pupils were then given time in lessons to decide how they would investigate the answers to their two questions. They were able to choose the methods used, the resources needed, the tasks for individual group members and the homework set (Strategy 4). It was important that, as part of this, pupils were involved in a dialogue (Strategy 5). This took various forms. Some groups wrote to Buddhist communities and then analysed the response they received in comparison to the "textbook" answer. Other groups spoke to Buddhist children in other year groups in the school. All groups were encouraged in each lesson to combine their work, through discussion, with pupils in the classroom who were investigating different areas of Buddhism. This helped them to build up a bigger picture of the tradition into which their questions fitted as a part (representation and interpretation).

Strategies 6 and 7 focus on elements of reflexivity. This was achieved when pupils wrote a final report on their investigation. For Strategy 6, pupils were asked to consider if they had learnt anything about their own ideas from their studies. Could they see any connections between their own ideas and those of Buddhism? One pupil considered the way in which the idea of nirvana in Buddhism and that of paradise in Islam appeared similar in some ways. Finally pupils were allowed to look back at their hypothesis. They were asked to analyse how accurate they had been in their initial ideas and to try to explain this. Had they drawn on knowledge about other faiths and applied this to Buddhism? Had they made accurate or inaccurate assumptions? The process allowed them to consider how they had used their knowledge of religious diversity and applied this to one specific tradition.

Adaptation of the learning approach

Throughout this work, pupils were involved in a process of moving inside and outside the religious tradition, making conceptual links and drawing on previous knowledge (representation and interpretation). Each individual pupil was challenged at a level appropriate to them – the boundaries for the task were removed and the work met the varying academic needs of the pupils. Pupils gained an emergent picture of the Buddhist tradition as well as engaging in a process of reflexivity between Buddhism and their own ideas. Classroom work utilised the skills of analysis, reflection, and investigation and proved engaging for all involved. Pupils showed increased motivation through their individualised learning and hermeneutical activities.

3. The dialogue approach

Albert Raasch

Introduction

As long as people are talking they are not making war. In this sense, dialogue is an educational instrument to avoid conflict – intercultural conflict in general and religious conflict in particular. The major role played by dialogue has given rise to an educational theory of dialogue, whose interdisciplinary nature reflects its many facets: religious, linguistic, social, ethical and so on. To clarify this role, we use a concept that has proved its value in discussions on intercultural communication in general and can therefore help to guide us through the interfaith dimension, which is simply one aspect of interculturalism, albeit an important one.

1. Functions of dialogue

According to this model, dialogue fulfils a number of functions that may be cumulative and are certainly not mutually exclusive. They constitute different aspects of a single whole, or to put it more accurately, dialogue goes through various stages. The model therefore reflects a dynamic process and can also help in teaching and learning dialogue. As such it is a practical educational tool and tries to clarify the objectives of any form of education aimed at securing peace, whether religious or other:

- dialogue that serves to discover others: their horizons, their values, their beliefs, etc.;

- dialogue that is also aimed at knowing oneself better, through comparison and interaction with another;

- based on the knowledge secured above, dialogue that helps acquire the skill of empathy, a highly valuable outcome and an essential precondition of the stages to follow;

- practical co-operation between faiths and among the adherents of different faiths, which is impossible without the empathy referred to in the third stage;

- going beyond mere co-operation, a further objective is to develop an identity both through and over and above all that separates religions; such an identity does not deny the differences that exist but emphasises what faiths have in common. The appropriate metaphor is that of sharing the same roof or umbrella as a way of finding shelter. In such cases, we can speak of a form of interfaith dialogue that, far from encouraging conflict and antagonism, goes beyond mere co-existence and promotes the community of people.

If it is to succeed, this process presupposes a more precise definition of "real" dialogue.

Partners in dialogue who seek to progress in the direction outlined above must listen to each other. This may go without saying but is nevertheless often not the case. Respect for the other person is a priority objective of the theory of dialogue.

2. Semantic features of dialogue

But dialogue requires more. It is necessary to understand the semantic features of the other's language. They must be analysed, so that they can be compared with the partner's own "dictionary". The partners must attempt, through a process of comparison, to arrive at a shared, or at least transparent, language as a basis on which they can understand and "accept" each other. This semantic work, which is eminently a task of the theory of dialogue, must be supplemented by a pragmatic or, better, pragmalinguistic dimension.

Pragmalinguistics sets out to define the relationship between a text as such and the function it serves, whether or not it is intended to. In concrete terms, the listener must not only ask what the other is saying but also what he wants to say, what is his intention or what are his intentions. The context must therefore be integrated into the interpretation of the words, a choice made between several possible interpretations and the current words combined with what has already been said and what will follow in the dialogue or communication. Account must be taken of the person speaking, and of social relationships with the person who is speaking/listening. Sense must be made of what remains implicit and unsaid, the often intentional ambiguities, the whole repertoire, in other words the strategies used by the other person in his part of the dialogue. Needless to say, the reverse process applies when it is the listener's turn to speak.

In order to understand the pragmatic function, it has to be borne in mind that everything that is said or expressed has a function in the dialogue vis-à-vis the other partner, in other words a social function. A dialogue is not a series of sentences but a sequence of statements or declarations. Each statement is an "act". And the term "function" also implies "effect". Those taking part in a dialogue are held responsible for what they say.

Learning how to enter into dialogue means learning to respect the other as a partner and accepting responsibility for achieving, in partnership with the other, a satisfactory conclusion to the dialogue. The "sense" or "meaning" of a statement has to be established through co-operation between the partners. A dialogue cannot be broken down into a series of isolated acts, but is an act in itself, a form of super-act, so to speak.

A dialogue that fails may signal the end of communication or even contact between persons. Dialogue is a social act with all the consequences, good or bad, that can be imagined. Dialogue is thus directed towards an outcome, takes place on various levels, and is structured in different stages. Dialogue is therefore a valuable tool in situations where the consequences of a failure to communicate between people and faiths are all too obvious.

2.1. Illustration: Pupil-to-pupil dialogue as a tool for religious education and for other subjects in the primary classroom

Julia Ipgrave, United Kingdom

Dialogical religious education

The pedagogical principles and strategies for a dialogical approach emerged from research on the religious and cultural influence of children from my school (in Leicester, England) on one another. Data were collected from a series of discussion events during which the young participants explored issues of faith and religious identity. Involvement in the research discussions stimulated the children's interest in religious questions, provided a safe forum for sharing issues that concerned them, provided them with opportunities to exercise their critical skills, gave underachievers a voice and encouraged a sense of moral seriousness as they tackled, and suggested their own solutions to, some of life's "big questions".

A threefold understanding of dialogue emerged from the project:

- Primary dialogue: the recognition of diversity and change, a daily encounter with different viewpoints, understandings and ideas.

- Secondary dialogue: a positive response to primary dialogue, openness to difference and to the possibility of being changed through encounter.

- Tertiary dialogue: the activity of dialogue itself; the forms and structures of verbal interchange that draw on primary and secondary dialogue.

Applying the dialogical approach to the classroom

Following the research project, this dialogical model was applied to the multicultural primary school where I worked and subsequently influenced developments in religious education in other Leicester schools. Applications of the threefold understanding of dialogue are set out below with examples from my own school practice (Ipgrave 2001, 2003).

Primary dialogue

- Acknowledging the diversity of experiences, viewpoints, understandings and ideas within the class.

- Using these as a resource for class discussions about beliefs and values.

- Introducing further viewpoints into classroom discussion.

The school where I introduced dialogical RE has a particularly diverse intake drawn from a variety of ethnic, religious and cultural backgrounds that became a resource for discussion. The children's experience of encounter with difference was extended further through interviews with visitors from other faith communities and by email partnerships set up with children from a suburban Roman Catholic school in the same city and from a primary school in more rural East Sussex. Material for discussion is introduced from several religious traditions. Other voices heard in the classroom include quotations from people holding a variety of beliefs or viewpoints or taking contrasting positions on moral issues debated by the children.

Secondary dialogue

- Promoting a class ethos in which children are willing to engage with difference, to share with and learn from others.
- Involving children in the establishment of principles for RE.
- Encouraging questioning to develop interest in others' experiences and points of view.

The children with whom I worked have had reason to be aware of the tensions that often accompany religious difference. International tensions (the wars in Afghanistan and Iraq, the Palestinian conflict and inter-communal troubles in Gujarat) affected local feelings among the various communities in the city. Against this background the children have been taught the skills of listening to and learning from others. In RE they were encouraged to discuss and set out the basic rules for the study of religions themselves. A class of nine and ten year-olds, for example, selected from their discussions three principles to guide their studies: respect for each other's religion; talking and thinking seriously about differences; being ready to learn new things "even about our own religion". These rules were revisited and used as success criteria when the pupils evaluated their learning at the end of lessons. Pupils are encouraged to formulate their own questions when they engage with other religions and viewpoints. They are also taught to try to view their own tradition from another's point of view. Muslim children, for example, were asked to view a video of the hajj pilgrimage as though they were visiting from another planet, to pick out elements they would find particularly strange and put together a list of questions they might ask.

Tertiary dialogue

- Employing a variety of methods, strategies and exercises to facilitate dialogue in the school.

- Structuring activities that encourage pupils to express views, negotiate and justify.

- Providing various stimuli to initiate and support discussion and debate (for example pictures, films, videos, case studies, stories, teachings from different traditions).

Children use sorting exercises in which they have to classify or sequence cards with different statements, words or pictures. As they do so they organise their thoughts, negotiate with each other and justify their choices. A class of eight-year-old children beginning a study of Islam were asked to find different ways to finish the statement, "A Muslim is someone who ..." In groups they then had to choose four of these to record on cards. All the statements were then shared and classified first under the headings "belief" and "practice" (leading to discussions about the relationship between the two) and then according to whether the statements applied only to Muslims or could also apply to various categories of non-Muslims. Another activity that helps children engage with different viewpoints is role-play, in which different groups or individuals have to argue a case from the point of view of a particular interest group. One case used in this way is the story of a man-eating tiger terrorising an Indian village where the children take on the roles of conservationist, tourist, mother, bereaved grandfather and government official as they debate whether or not the tiger should be hunted and killed.

Dialogue beyond the classroom

A dialogical approach to RE has been successfully extended beyond the classroom to promote interreligious and intercultural understanding by email between pupils from a number of primary schools in contrasting regions of the UK. Using a model of interfaith dialogue by email developed in two Leicester schools, inner city schools have linked up with suburban schools, city schools with rural schools, largely "white" schools with schools that are ethnically mixed. Individual children communicate by email with their partner in the school with which theirs is twinned. The exchanges between the children follow a structured schedule that is tied in with the religious education schemes of work used at the two schools. Questions and ideas from RE lessons are fed into the email dialogue and material from the exchanges in turn is used to feed further discussion in class.

The dialogue progresses through four stages:

- Introduction: making friends, discussing interests and hobbies, favourite TV programmes and football teams.

- Sharing experience: finding out about each other's family traditions and religious practices.

- Questions of faith: discussing their beliefs about some key questions such as life after death, the existence of angels, the beginning of the world.

- Ethical debate: engaging in moral debate about issues such as the use of violence, the rights of animals, gambling.

In some cases the schools have been able to build on the friendships developing between their pupils to organise other activities for intercultural meetings including exchanges of assemblies, sports activities in a city park and shared residential trips. For two years running children from the predominantly Muslim Leicester school and their Roman Catholic friends have shared a places of worship day on which Muslim children guided their Christian friends round their mosque and the Christian children guided their Muslim friends round their church. After the tours the children then got together in the school ICT suites to produce jointly electronic guides to the two places of worship. The children's own words give their views on the success of the email dialogue in promoting positive intercultural understanding:

- "[The project] made Christians seem like real people. We use different names for our gods and prophets but it's the same god and some of our prophets are the same" (Muslim child, Leicester).

- "We've really enjoyed it because we have been able to communicate with children who are far away and have different beliefs" (Christian child, East Sussex).

4. The contextual approach

Heid Leganger-Krogstad

Introduction

It is a fact that all education is contextual. Is there then a need for a contextual approach to education? Would not a more universal approach fit better in times of globalisation? A global approach could presumably promote shared values through common knowledge and could possibly create a better understanding among humans. Or is it rather the opposite? A contextual approach takes into account the fact that knowledge is contextually bound and that every person looks at life from a different viewpoint and cannot be free from this unless by conscious effort. A contextual approach is about investigating the spectacles that culture gives humans to look at the world through. Global understanding is considered to be a main objective in the contextual approach, but it suggests a different way than some sort of universal or European approach to achieve this common goal.

1. Globalisation

Globalisation is making the world simultaneously smaller and bigger. The world becomes smaller as the globe becomes a common sphere of human interaction across national and cultural boundaries, but it becomes much bigger in terms of the peoples and places on the map that impose themselves on our European consciousness. On the one hand, there is interconnectedness and unifying effects, on the other hand independence and fragmentation.

The new information technologies create an information society removing the former problem of lack of information. Now the overload of information creates new possibilities, challenges and even problems. It becomes more and more obvious that holding information is not the same thing as having knowledge. The main challenge today is how to equip children and young people not just with knowledge but knowledge upon which they can act. How can we give them competence for their present and future lives?

Research done on the younger generation in the information society characterises this generation as "glocal" (Brunstad 1998, pp. 129-137). "Glocal" is a new verbal construction, a combination of "global" and "local". It refers to the fact that young people have global information and are shaped by the global market, but at the same time they define their own local world. Young people's sense of responsibility does not extend far beyond their personal life project. They take responsibility for their individual lifestyle, identity formation, and career building, and for their family and friends, but their responsibility includes neither their neighbours and neighbourhood nor the region and the nation. They seem overwhelmed by the problems of the global world and tend to solve this by defining a more practicable individual life project. This might also be an explanation for the lack of social and political interest among youth today, according to Brunstad.

The result of an endless multitude of possibilities and expectations is a paralysed attitude towards global challenges, an attitude that is widespread also in older generations. How can we educate future generations for citizenship and global awareness under such conditions? How can we help them to "think globally and act locally"?

There is no contradiction between the contextual approach and the global aim. Global awareness is shown in local action. Being a caring parent for your biological children, for instance, does not mean you are less capable of also caring for children in the neighbourhood or are less interested in long-distance child sponsorship. Global awareness is taught and learned through recognising the difference between local and global factors in the local environment. If something really is global, then it also affects every tiny locality. In a contextual approach, one begins with simple and local structures and moves on to those that are more complex. According to this theory, competence in social studies is developed first by relating to simple structures in the local society, followed by an understanding of the interaction between local society and the greater context. The long-term goal is that pupils develop competence in understanding co-operation and interaction in a global society.

2. Contextuality

Contextuality is regarded both as a fact and as a programme. All education is contextual in the sense that it is formed by its contextual conditions. These contextual factors are partly explicit and expressed but mainly implicit in social systems and cultures, and as such seldom expressed in words. In traditional and mainly monocultural societies this functions well, but not in societies with rapid changes and high mobility. The increasing religious and cultural diversity in Europe makes it necessary to verbalise the implicit values and ideas, in order to make them open for discussion. Contextual factors such as geographical, historical and social structures, ethnic, religious and cultural factors, school systems and educational politics, need to be analysed and described. Such descriptions of the implicit factors have as an aim to make education more transparent and open for minority groups in society. Transparency is a precondition for public debate and for a democratic negotiation about values and ideas in education.

This need became obvious in the northernmost county in Norway where this contextual approach was first developed (Leganger-Krogstad 2000). The two minority cultures in this society, the Kven and the Sámi cultures, had until 15 years ago nearly no influence on educational content or values, and were in need of having their voice heard (Leganger-Krogstad 1998). The contextual theory is inspired by Paulo Freire's Pedagogy of the Oppressed (1996) and makes use of a mixture of the praxis and anthropological models for contextual theology (Bevans 1992). The religious and cultural conditions in the region were studied and described to provide school authorities, teachers and teacher students with more adequate knowledge about the cultural and religious conditions in the region (Kristiansen 1996, Leganger-Krogstad 1995). It was a challenge for educational authorities to facilitate the empowerment of these minority parents through displaying a higher degree of transparency in their educational policy. This shows in general that there is a need for a system where minorities can make their voices heard and where the majority in power are obliged to include cultural diversity in their curriculum and educational practice. Working to minimise the hidden curriculum in every school is a main goal. This includes willingness to verbalise the contextual factors deciding educational praxis in the particular school.

Education in Norway, as in many other countries, has been built on a long monocultural, Christian tradition. Even though Norway still has limited experience with direct multi-religious reality, the indirect influence of a globalised world makes thorough changes in educational thinking necessary. This transformation process started in Norway in the 1980s. The national curriculum has for a long time given the local schools considerable leeway for local adaptations to the present cultural diversity. In spite of this, however, local adaptation has not been part of the normal school life, especially not in religious education. Teachers have felt the need for the support the textbooks have offered when meeting different groups of pupils and parents. The textbooks have been and still are very influential, and thus a common national curriculum is practised to a high degree in most classrooms.

3. Learning in a local culture

The contextual approach aims at making use of the experiences children have from life outside school, from their backgrounds and in their local communities. These experiences are often very vague and uninformed, but they are extremely valuable for educational use. Knowledge can be built on them, and this is relevant knowledge since it is linked to their own life-world. Schools aim at equipping children with competence for life in their own local communities. They are taught how to look for and recognise treasures of religious thinking and action in their own societies. If the children have few experiences of recognising religion when they come to school, it is a task for the school to show them where religion has influenced thinking and behaviour, history and culture in their nearest environments. By creating common meeting places, schools can give the children common experiences that increase their ability for detecting religion. The cultural context is the environment for education, the educational content and the life-world in which they are to achieve life competence (Afdal, Haakedal and Leganger-Krogstad 1997).

According to a contextual approach each particular socio-cultural context has some features, some common history, material cultural artefacts, rituals, festivals or celebrations, or some problems and challenges to address, that can serve as a common ground for education. A contextual approach is based on a socio-cultural idea about learning and emphasises the need for learning processes in authentic settings (Vygotsky 1987). Authentic settings are more complex than the school settings, but in meeting them, children with different learning abilities can cope more according to their own interests. Collaboration between school and society is a precondition, however.

One of the challenges in a contextual approach is the need for co-operation between academics and schools to reveal the implicit factors in the educational structures and in culture; another challenge is helping schools recognise the religious features in the local community. A contextual approach has to be developed differently in every context (Valk 2002; Heimbrock 2004). In order to keep local material from being embraced narrow-mindedly, it needs to be seen in a broader context and be evaluated and criticised by a national curriculum and international standards.

Contextual approaches are useful in all school subjects. The contextual approach to religious education makes use of theory from contextual theology to investigate religion as it is expressed in the context where education takes place. Religion, as an empirical phenomenon and not primarily as a normative phenomenon, is the centre of interest. Religion can be studied in books, and it can also be studied in contemporary culture. This approach gives value to religion as it is displayed in the everyday life of humans, in common values, in habits and traditions, and also through history and in the cultural environment. The main objective in this approach is to help the pupils achieve competence in recognising religious expressions and religious features displayed in their local community and how this locality is interlinked with other parts of the globe and is influenced by global developments.

A contextual approach to religious education focuses on the concrete and the particular, and less on the abstract and general. It focuses on religious life and less on religious doctrine. The pupils' socio-cultural environment is regarded as more important for the early learning process than the textbooks, and local adaptation of the national curriculum is necessary in order to reach educational aims.

3.1. Illustration 1: The School and Community Project

Heid Leganger-Krogstad, Norway

Introduction

The school as an institution tends to live its own life partly separated from the community. Schools need to be safe and protective arenas for children, but separatism from the community is not a desirable side-effect. When school is opened up towards the wider world, it leads to education for citizenship. Overall aims for education in Norway is that the school shall:

> 10. make it possible to co-operate with the homes of the pupils and ensure that parents/guardians can have joint responsibility in the school;

> 11. make it possible for the local community to become involved in education in a meaningful way (The Learning Poster).[10]

The Norwegian Parliament decided that The Learning Poster should be very clear on the need for parental influence. Co-operation with the parents and the local community has always been important, but in these days when parents have "less time" and the voluntary sector gets smaller, politicians have an interest in maintaining local communities through their schools. Non-formal education is an important part of a child's upbringing. The ideal of giving parents influence and opportunities for co-operation in the school is not always easy to realise in different school settings.

Participation in the community is an overall objective for education, and how to participate is taught through continuous involvement in the school's neighbourhood. Schools play a key role in this learning process, and nearly all the children in Norwegian communities belong to the Norwegian public school system, as very few private schools exist in Norway. A school then mirrors the diversity in the society where it is situated, both the richness and the conflicts. It is an educational aim to support the development of the pupils' concern for the wider world. The contextual approach gives priority to learning in authentic settings, and learning through direct encounters with others. This might be between different schools, between generations, between professions, between different school subjects, between religions, between the secular and the religious, and between school and society.

---

10. The educational reform called Knowledge Promotion, implemented in 2006, has this Learning Poster as a list of 11 key principles in education: http://www.stortinget.no/inns/2003/200304-268-002.html.

A school and community project takes place every year in a community situated in a valley outside Oslo, Lommedalen in Bærum. This community has some suburban features due to a relatively fast expansion from 350 to 11 000 inhabitants over a period of 15 years. Owing to this expansion, the community lacks stability. A small minority of the inhabitants have a long and rooted history in the valley; the majority, however, hardly have any conscious local identity. The location has many material signs of its history through many old buildings from the 1600s that have been properly taken care of by the family which succeeds the first ironworks owners. The history of this ironworks is established and part of the potential for the educational project.

For 10 years this school and community project has been an established tradition, bringing the children and youth together with their parents, grandparents, friends and neighbours, where they can present the results of their educational process concerning the major theme of the year (Leganger-Krogstad 2003). The name and traditions of an almost forgotten festival is used in this co-operative educational project, because of its dia-logical potential: St Michael's mass is used because of the tradition's emphasis on open gates between people in a community.

St Michael's Mass as a common meeting place

*   St Michael is a common angel in three religions.
*   St Michael's Mass is celebrated "to open the gates" between people.

St Michael is the most ecumenical of angels as he originates in Jewish tra-dition and appears in the Christian and in the Islamic tradition. St Michael is an archangel in all the three religions, "a safeguard against the wicked-ness and snares of the devil".[11] Concerning the traditions, in the autumn, on 29 September, the crops were harvested and the farm animals were to be

11. In 1994 Pope John Paul II requested the faithful to take up again the Prayer to St Michael, as part of the battle of our times "against the forces of darkness and against the spirit of this world". The Pope said: "May prayer strengthen us for the spiritual battle we are told about in the Letter to the Ephesians: 'Draw strength from the Lord and from his mighty power' (Eph 6:10). The Book of Revelation refers to this same battle recalling before our eyes the image of St Michael the Archangel (Rev. 12:7). Pope Leo XIII certainly had a very vivid recollection of this scene when, at the end of the last century, he introduced a special prayer to St Michael throughout the Church: 'St Michael the Archangel defend us in battle, be our safe-guard against the wickedness and snares of the devil.' Although today this prayer is no lon-ger recited at the end of Mass, I ask everyone not to forget it, and to recite it to obtain help in the battle against the forces of darkness and against the spirit of this world." [Pope John Paul II, Regina Caeli, 24 April 1994] http://www.ewtn.com/expert/answers/st_michael_prayer.htm.

safely brought into the cowshed before winter time. When the animals were safe, the farmers could leave the gates open, making it possible for the neighbours to visit one another without climbing fences.

St Michael's Mass is an education programme that takes place in the autumn every year. The tradition started 10 years ago, after an initiative taken by the local congregation of the Church of Norway, when its new church building was raised in the middle of the local community. The congregation wanted to mark its open door policy by inviting all the schools in the neighbourhood to a common project.[12] The church is situated next to the school where all the pupils meet for lower secondary education after having done their primary education in four different smaller schools. Each year a new central theme is chosen for the school's work. It is approached from different perspectives and on different levels, with the purpose of learning and presenting results as part of a festival on an Open School Saturday that takes place both in the church and at the secondary school. The theme that serves as a point of departure each year needs to have some local relevance in order to create a common ground of interest. This co-operative educational project has the goal of opening the gates between institutions in the neighbourhood: between the school and the church, between the different schools, between the generations, between different school subjects, between religions, between the secular and the religious, and between school and society.

The programme committee consisting of representatives from church, school and community decides on some artists in residence to visualise the major topic, and they co-operate with the children in a process where they learn some of the techniques in use and make their artistic expressions. They also decide the major topic and provide expertise for the teaching that prepares for the Open School Day – the highlight of St Michael's mass. This takes place on a Saturday close to St Michael's patron day, 29 September. The tradition of celebrating St. Michael's mass is almost lost in the evangelical Lutheran church to which most Norwegians belong.[13] However, the National Council within the Church of Norway is making efforts to renew this tradition.[14] On the Open School Day the pupils show the results of their work on the major topic on an outdoor stage, in the school yard and in the classrooms where many parallel sessions take place.

---

12. If there were other religious institutions in this local community, they would have been included. There exists no mosque, synagogue or temple.
13. Membership: 3.88 million – 85.7% of the population.
14. http://www.kirken.no/Besluttende_organer/nyhetDet.cfm?pNyhetId=54&pNyhetKat=4&pVedtakId=49.

The committee provides for some supervision and assistance to the teaching by engaging some professionals, local artists, photographers, painters, choreographers, actors or musicians. This is done in order to give extra inspiration to the teaching and learning of the major topic. The professionals assist either the teachers or the pupils directly in the exploration process through drama, creative work on posters or sculptures, singing or music, and other diverse activities. Connected to the theme, a combined amateur and professional cultural programme is planned to create events that bring the generations together in church. This includes concerts, exhibitions, events and lectures. Through open lectures different dialogical themes concerning world religions have been addressed.

The major topics

The major topics must be of relevance for several school subjects; only then is it obvious for teachers how they can be dealt with in a cross-curricular way. During the years the major themes have been as follows: Fairytales; Folk songs; Autumn and harvesting; Females in local history; A particular author; The second millennium: Jesus; My home; and Norway 1905-2005 – a comparison. In 2005 Norway celebrated the anniversary of the peaceful dissolution of the union with Sweden in 1905. The purpose of this anniversary is "to take a fresh look at the history, values and possibilities of our country, with an aim to see Norwegians as citizens of the world". The discussion on a national level concerning Multicultural Norway took up questions such as: Whose heritage is included in our "national" history, and how are "Norway" and the "Norwegian" constructed today? Linked to these questions and from a multicultural perspective, the pupils can study the diverse roots and contributions to present society in such subjects as language, history, social studies, science and environment, arts and crafts, music, home economics and physical training. The religious dimension can be addressed by looking at the cultural roots of Christianity, from Hebrew/Greek tradition, with Egyptian, Syrian, Babylonian and Roman elements. The long history of Christianity before it influenced Norway could also be studied. Meeting points between religions in history and the ecumenical potential in common roots can also be addressed. This can lead up to a discussion on whether the Norwegian nation of today can be referred to as Christian or not. A lesson on the use of terminology in a multicultural society can be included, to help the pupils learn the difference between exclusive and inclusive language concerning religion.

In the year 2000, when Jesus was the major theme, the children worked on icons in different ways. The older students were taught the orthodox painting technique from a professional icon painter, and the younger ones learned how to make theirs on paper or on glass. The oldest students were asked to present Jesus of today in a sculpture using available cheap material. "How do we know Jesus?", "Jesus as both human and God", "incarnation", "images of Jesus today", and "Jesus as part of Islamic tradition" were all themes included in this project.

Another year a famous choreographer worked with the children on their fairytale performances, and professional folk dancers worked with the children when folk songs were the major theme. The idea is that this co-operative effort between teachers and professionals provided by the church, preferably local artists if there are any available for the purpose, inspires in the teachers new ideas for teaching.

In the church there is a yearly exhibition where the artist's and the pupils' work are exhibited together. An example: photos of homes in the suburbs taken by the pupils were edited on the computer. The photographer taught them the editing technique and discussed the choice of motifs with them. He helped them discover typical features in their own homes, a selection of items to photograph, and had them comment on their choices in writing. The younger children made drawings on "The home of my dreams". Others investigated the questions "Why do I feel at home in my own house?" as well as: "Where is my second home?" It is possible to add other questions to this: "What is the difference between different homes?" "What are the common traits between my home and yours?" "What makes the church a home for those who gather there?" "To what extent do I feel at home in my church / my mosque / my synagogue / my temple?" "How is the theme 'home' used in different holy texts?"

Adaptation of a contextual approach

A contextual approach is useful where there is a lack of textbooks or other teaching material in the educational system. To investigate religion in the local context through a mixture of historical material, facts and empirical religion or culture, is often an eye-opener for children towards the religious dimension of everyday life. Examples could be the calendar of the society, the week, traditions in the house, clothing, the food we eat, rules for what is classified as food, food for festivals, greetings, traditions for names of humans and streets, schools and hospitals, the organisation of family life, cosmology, ethics and values, buildings, art and symbols. Religion is displayed through the cultural environment in many ways, but it is often necessary to focus on a religious perspective to be able to see it. Pupils often need to take part in an educational process supervised by the teacher or other adults or professionals to know what to look for. All this can be investigated from a religious perspective.

The religious dimension in the project about fairytales can be done like this: Different cultures share folk tales with common themes. Fairytales are closely linked to religious traditions. The same folk tale may exist in different versions due to the cultural context of its telling. How do our fairytales look, and do we know of any fairytale to compare with from other cultural settings?

Folk songs have religious motifs and reflect religious interpretations in former times. What do they tell about the religious life of former generations? Females in former times can help the pupils understand their own situation in a historic light. Insight into old traditional customs and ethical rules can add perspectives to the understanding of religious traditions as they reappear in contemporary society.

St Michael's Mass is an old tradition, but not too fixed and rooted. This means it can be open for renewed use and new traditions. Schools can make use of this ecumenical and dialogical angel that stands for an open door policy in their own locality in their own way to create a meeting place in the local community.

3.2. Ilustration 2: Becoming a guest in a festival of the Other
Peter Schreiner

Introduction

Many schools in Europe recognise and integrate into their teaching and school life festivals of religions that are familiar to some (at least) of the pupils and their families. Festivals can build bridges between people of different faiths. This is mainly done in primary schools taking into account that festivals have a great significance for pupils that belong to a religious tradition.

There are some pedagogical reasons to do that. Younger pupils especially appreciate that highlights of their life are recognised in school. For older pupils festivals can be used to discuss the value of a religious practice, the relationship between society, religion and the private sphere, and the relevance of a religion in society.

The importance of festivals

Festivals are important for several reasons.

- Our own practice of festivals can also open up to us an entrance to the festivals of others, taking into account similarities and differences.

- By introducing and celebrating "own" festivals and festivals of "others" we should be honest not only about their beauty and interest but also how they may be strange or annoying.

- The main focus is the people who celebrate a feast. Festivals provide excellent opportunities for first encounter and then dialogue. Knowledge about festivals plays an important role for the living together of neighbours.

Celebrating festivals

The acknowledgement of a festival can be done in different ways. In some cases calendars of religious festivals are in the classroom and teachers have discussed the importance of some of the festivals with pupils and/or their parents. The Shap[15] working party in England has a long-standing tradition of the production of a calendar of religious festivals. The calendar includes information about festivals of the main religious traditions in England and Wales and is available also in a pictorial version. A European adaptation of

---

15. www.shap.org.uk.

this calendar is available through the European Association for World Religions in Education[16] (EAWRE).

Encouraging openness for the diversity of religions and worldviews can be a guideline and objective for including religious festivals in the teaching and learning process or as an element of the broader school life. Dealing with religious festivals can provide opportunities for pupils to recognise the richness of diverse cultures in their own tradition and to put their own experiences in a wider context. It seems to be important not to use or misuse pupils as representatives of a specific religious tradition in the sense of making them experts of this tradition. The celebration of a festival in the classroom should create a feeling of a common activity. However, the relation to the specific festival can and will be different. Many schools have already developed a "tradition" of festivals, for example including the Islamic festival of breaking the fast alongside more secular events of some Christian festivals. In each of the main religions there is also a festival that is most well-known and appreciated or others that have a central importance for the religion. In a school term, a series of festivals can be acknowledged and integrated into school life, such as children's festivals, birthdays of religious founders, New Year's festivals or important holy events for each of the religions.

Festivals of different religions can be used for sharing experiences of pupils. Pupils may agree on an area where they do a kind of fast, for example a period without watching TV. They could work out a grid where pupils note their "success". In this period it is important to organise meetings to share experiences and also failures.

Although not all pupils in a multi-religious class can say: "This is a festival of my tradition," it is important to add to the common element of celebrating a festival a more specific one for those who belong to its religious tradition. Learning can happen then in a movement between common shared experiences and individual experiences. When celebrating festivals it might be helpful to imagine a situation where neighbours invite each other to a festival. When a Muslim family invites a Christian family to fast-breaking at the end of Ramadan it is obvious that they are the host and the others the guest; they are familiar with it, the others show uncertainty. When a festival is celebrated in a class the whole class participates; however, it is not everyone's festival, so different roles exist. Also here you have hosts and guests. This should be taken into consideration in the preparation process.

---

16. www.eawre.org.

**Key points of a contextual approach
and the school and community project: St Michael's Mass**

The contextual approach:

- uses a common feature or a meeting place in the cultural environment as a basis for inter-religious and intercultural learning;

- is based on a socio-cultural idea about learning and emphasises the need for learning processes in authentic settings;

- recognises that each particular socio-cultural context has some features, some common history, material cultural artefacts, rituals, festivals or celebrations, or some problems and challenges to address, that can serve as a common ground for education;

- is especially useful where there is a lack of textbooks or other teaching material in the educational system.

St Michael is a common angel in three religions, hence St Michael's Mass has dialogical potential and an emphasis on an open door policy between people in a community, between institutions in the neighbourhood, between the school and the church, the synagogue and the mosque (when possible), between the different schools, between the generations, between different school subjects, between professions, between the religions, between the secular and the religious, and between school and society.

Key points in becoming a guest in the festival of the Other

- Religious festivals can be brought to the classroom to build bridges between people of different faiths.

- Encouraging openness for the diversity of religions and worldviews can be a guideline and objective for including religious festivals in the teaching and learning process or as an element of the broader school life.

- Dealing with religious festivals can provide opportunities for pupils to recognise the richness of diverse cultures in their own tradition, to put their own experiences in a wider context, and discover similarities and differences.

PART III

WHOLE SCHOOL ISSUES
OF INTERCULTURAL EDUCATION
AND THE RELIGIOUS DIMENSION

John Keast and Heid Leganger-Krogstad

Introduction

This third part of the reference book focuses on the supportive environment for teachers in their classroom practice. It deals with the importance of educational policies, teacher training, school management and classroom practice. Part II describes approaches for handling religious diversity in positive and dialogical ways in the classroom setting. Practice inside the classroom, however, cannot be separated from the life of the school itself. The values of the school as an educational institution in society, and in a particular school, form the basis of rules for classroom practice. The values in a particular school might, in a diverse Europe, be decided on a national, regional and/or local level in the educational system. School systems are closely related to the religious landscape of a particular country. Parallel school systems according to religious divisions are common. In former monocultural societies the normal situation was that the state or the church was the owner of the school, and the nature of the school expressed religious or ideological values in accordance with this ownership.

In increasingly plural societies reconsideration of the values base for the school system is a prerequisite for giving religious minorities their human rights and children the competence needed for life in a global world. Negotiations to define the common values a school needs for the future should be conducted on a national or regional level in respect of religious traditions and history, and in dialogue with religious communities.

1. The learning environment

Educational policies, school governance and the identity of the school have a decisive impact on the practice in a particular classroom. The practice of individual teachers is, to a large extent, shaped by influences from colleagues in their school. Collectively they formulate a type of common understanding according to which they live their professional lives. The days of the solo playing teacher are long gone. The collective theory of practice forms the identity of the school and, since it is often formulated in less pluralistic societies, it can be challenged in contemporary society. The identity of most schools needs to be reformulated to include and to value religious diversity. The religious dimension in education has to be addressed in school development planning in a more conscious way in the future. This means that policy makers at all levels and the governance of educational institutions are to be included in this process of rethinking the values base of education, particularly in a global society. Part I of this reference book gives the theoretical basis for such a rethinking process.

For too long the religious dimension has been neglected in education due to the problem of finding common ground. By focusing on religious diversity as mainly problematic rather than enriching, policymakers can increase rather than solve difficulties. Cultural diversity cannot be addressed without including religion. Religious diversity as part of Education for Democratic Citizenship is also part of a common interest among scholars in religious education and the Council of Europe. In the approach taken to intercultural learning through the policies of the Council of Europe and the European Commission (Intercultural Learning T-Kit 2000), the task has been to create a positive environment for intercultural and interreligious education (The religious dimension of intercultural education 2004). The school environment involves the level of policy, school governance, school leadership and management, curriculum construction and co-ordination, and teacher training. Outside the educational system parents, religious communities, NGOs and community organisations are also important partners in creating such an environment for learning.

2. Promoting the valuing of religious diversity in different educational settings

Valuing diversity and learning to live with religious differences can happen in many ways in schools and colleges. There are obvious different types of diversity. One type is educational – with pupils exhibiting special needs to be met or having talented gifts that need to be developed. Another is social diversity, with pupils of different socio-economic groups. Ethnic diversity is another obvious form, with diversity of language and cultures. Among such diversity may be religious diversity, but not always so. Cultural and religious diversity are not the same, as a single religion has followers from many cultural backgrounds. This reference book focuses on religious diversity, with pupils of different beliefs, practices, expression and values, and on the kind of religious dialogue necessary in a global society.

3. Phases and settings

First, valuing diversity can happen at all phases of education, from the youngest of children through to adult education and lifelong learning. Arguably, education in the early years is the most formative, and so adults who work with young children have a particularly potent opportunity for effective developing of the skills and attitudes needed by children to value diversity. For example, the kinds of toys, stories, and other resources used in early years education can enable children to become familiar with a range of diverse artefacts and promote diversity as normal; and the kinds of experiences of other adults and children and places visited can also have a similar effect.

At compulsory school level, the same kinds of opportunities are available, though in rather different ways according to the age of the pupils. Colleges of higher education and universities can replicate these also, though the context and nature of the opportunities will vary.

All the phases described above may be found in faith and non-faith settings (that is, schools and colleges with or without a religious character). The valuing of diversity should occur in both. Whatever the advantages or disadvantages that each kind of setting has, the education of children and young people in a faith institution does not have to be of a narrow, mono-cultural or exclusive kind. It is in the interests of faith- and non-faith-based institutions to promote the valuing of diversity among their young people. Of prime importance is the quality of what happens in the various aspects of education, irrespective of setting and phase. This is what determines how effective the promotion of valuing diversity is. Such valuing needs to be the result of the different aspects of education being consistent and mutually reinforcing. Inconsistent messages undermine the coherence of the education to value diversity and promote dialogue.

4. School ethos

First, the very ethos of the institution is important, as it is from this that the overall climate and environment of the education takes its tone. If the values espoused by the institution are not respectful of diversity and encouraging of respecting and valuing diversity, then it is unlikely that such forms of education will flourish in the life of the institution or in the curriculum. This means that all those who create and maintain the ethos of an institution are involved and who are responsible for the foundation and management of the institution. In the UK, this would include the governors (and through them the parents and the wider community whom they both represent and influence) and the staff, both teaching and non-teaching. Apart from the people, the organisational systems themselves that host and portray the values are important.

Positive values such as accurate knowledge and non-stereotyping, respect and courtesy, valuing the individual, family and community, non-discrimination and harassment, positive acceptance of various traditions and difference – all these are the foundation of the right ethos.

5. School policies

Second, the policies of the institution are important as they help to remove the space in which diversity can be devalued. The admissions policy, for example, which may be discriminatory in different ways depending on the nature and type of the institution, should be openly shared and fairly implemented. The policies on behaviour and bullying, personal and social development need to be sensitive, shared and known by all.

6. School governance

Third, the actual life and practices of the institution are very powerful, as these either set a positive example, and show how the ethos and policies are properly implemented, or they betray the hypocrisy of practice over preaching. Most children learn most powerfully by example, especially when young, so the day-to-day life of the institution has an enormous effect on how diversity may be valued. The aspects of life that are particularly important in valuing religious diversity and dialogue are any arrangements for religious practice and worship, the actual learning environment in the school public areas and displays, the library and resources available, the use of the diversity in the school community and its involvement with it, the administration of policy, and the quality of the relationships between staff themselves, and between staff and pupils. How far the institution engages with diversity in its community is also a good indicator of how much it values such diversity.

7. School curriculum

Fourth, the curriculum is also important, for it is here that the opportunities for staff and pupils to actually study the issues raised by valuing religious diversity and dialogue are to be found. If there are none, then value would be nil. If there are few, or they are sporadic, tokenistic or negative, then the value will be undermined. If they are coherent, and the curriculum offers a width of relevant learning opportunities, such as in religious education, the humanities, citizenship, and others like literature and the arts, then the curriculum will complement the ethos and support it.

Faith settings will have a positive advantage and interest in promoting understanding of religious diversity and dialogue since it is of the teaching of most faiths to respect those who believe differently even if they are felt to be wrong. Because faith settings are usually the result of putting religious values into practice, then the ethos, life, and curriculum of such settings should be particularly sensitive to the needs for valuing religious diversity and promoting dialogue. The way in which this is done may be different from a non-faith setting because of the context, history and nature of the institution, but being a faith setting does not mean that issues of religious diversity and dialogue are irrelevant or unimportant.

8. A checklist of key issues and questions for self-reflection and for action

This checklist of key issues and questions for self-reflection is meant to help different partners to identify their role in creating the right environment for teaching and learning.

8.1. Ethos and values

- What is the values base of the school or college?
- Who defines and promotes it?
- Does it encourage and promote dialogue and respect?
- Does it reflect the religious dimension of intercultural education?
- Are these values publicised and agreed with parents and the community?
- How far are intercultural education values part of the general vision or aim for the school?

8.2. Educational policies

- Does the admissions policy of the school take account of diverse needs of pupils and the community?
- How far do the policies on behaviour, bullying, personal and social development promote the values of intercultural education, the value of religious diversity and respect?

8.3. School governance and management

- How far does school governance and management reflect the value of diversity?
- How far is the school's tradition based on the dominant religion in the state?
- How far does the school calendar reflect religious diversity?
- To what extent do holidays reflect the diversity of religious holy days?
- Are there common days of celebration, based on common humanity, for example UN day?
- How does the selection of holidays reflect the religions represented by the teachers and the student body in the school?
- How does the school organise the need for the different religions' holy days?
- To what extent does the food provided in school reflect the diversity of cultures and needs?
- How is the wearing of particular clothing or religious symbols dealt with?
- To what extent does it reflect the diversity of pupils in the school?
- How is conflict resolution achieved if necessary?

8.4. The curriculum

- Has the school conducted an audit of its provision of intercultural education, and its religious dimension?
- Is the curriculum one where tradition dominates over modernity?
- How far does the curriculum cater for the future needs of the children?
- How is cultural diversity studied? In what areas? How effectively?
- Does philosophical or/and ethical study provide for religious diversity? How effective is this?
- How is the spiritual, moral, social and cultural development of each pupil provided?
- How far does citizenship deal with intercultural education and religious diversity?
- Whose language dominates the education provided?
- To what extent does the history taught in the school mirror all the cultures present?
- Whose music is played during the school day?

- Whose games are played in the school yard?
- Whose sports are part of the school curriculum?

8.5. Religious education (where provided)

- Is religious education offered as a separate school subject? How effective is this?
- Is religious education integrated into other school subjects? How effective is this?
- Which religions are presented in religious education? Why?
- Is religious education a responsibility of the school or given in co-operation with religious communities?
- How far is the dominant religion viewed as the only truth and as a normative perspective?
- To what extent is the child's own religious background seen as normative?
- To what extent are all religions viewed as equally searching for truth?
- Is every child's spiritual development seen as the purpose for religious education?
- Are the common features between religions emphasised?
- Is there a critical attitude to religions?
- Are religions taught and discussed in separate classrooms?
- Are all religions presented side by side without preferences of any kind (multi-religious systematic approach)?
- Are all the religions presented side by side without preferences in quality but in quantity?
- Is comparative religious education based on common themes for the religions?
- Is interreligious dialogue based in respect for differences?

8.6. Training

- To what extent have teachers been trained to provide a religious dimension in intercultural education?
- What opportunities are there for teachers to gain such training? To what extent are these opportunities taken up?

PART IV

EXAMPLES OF CURRENT PRACTICE

Introduction

This section of the reference book includes some examples of current practice across Europe's schools. This is obviously very varied, and reflects the different educational systems and structures of member states, their histories and traditions and their religious and cultural composition.

It is important to realise that the examples included in this section of the reference book are not offered as examples of good practice. These examples of current practice were not written for inclusion in this reference book, but simply represent what is going on in different places in Europe. Thus, the examples are very varied, and some are better than others. They are not all based on the principles and methodologies of this reference book, and should not therefore be read as such, though aspects of the examples given will illustrate some of these. So, if the examples are not offered as specific illustrations of good practice, why have they been included in this reference book? The examples are given because they have some usefulness deriving from their very variety of kind, context, and quality.

First, the examples represent the wide range of opportunities for schools to deal with religious diversity and intercultural education. This includes the use of national language and cultural programmes, the use of well-known or important texts in a particular member state, the use of education outside the classroom by children visiting museums or places of importance to religious and other believers, the use of the creative arts including music, cultural exchanges where students encounter other students in their own context, the use of specific activities or occasions in the life of a school to focus on intercultural matters, and use of work with local and faith communities, as well as classroom teaching and learning on religious diversity. The range is not complete, but it is hoped that the examples given will encourage teachers to look across the wide range of potential opportunities in their own schools and extend their own practices.

Second, the examples illustrate the scale of opportunities, from national programmes organised by government to local events organised by one or two individuals in schools and their community. Similarly, the examples illustrate activities that take a shorter or a longer period of time to prepare and to implement. It is important to remember that religious diversity and intercultural education can take place at different levels within any education system, and come in different sizes. Schools should not feel that they are unable to do anything even if they think that there is a lack of opportunity nationally or regionally, or if they only have short periods of time to use.

Third, the examples vary in the extent to which the religious dimension of intercultural education is explicit or implicit. Some examples focus clearly on knowledge and understanding of religion and try to develop skills of evaluation and application. Other examples raise the religious dimension within the context of a historical, linguistic, artistic or textual study. Schools are encouraged to look across the subjects of the curriculum and realise their potential to deal with the religious dimension of intercultural education.

Fourth, the variety of quality contained within these examples enables teachers to reflect critically upon the practice of others and apply their thinking to their own practice. Questions such as:

- How effective is this example of practice?
- Does it actually fulfil what it sets out to do? If not, why not?
- How could I improve this example?
- What would I have to do to make it possible for me to use it?

This is not an exhaustive list of questions, but it indicates the kind of professional approach to the practice of others that can help one teacher learn from that practice.

To enable such critical reflection, it is important to refer back to the concepts and methodological sections of this reference book, as they provide the source and criteria for such reflection. Teachers might like to ask themselves to what extent the examples given:

- run the risk of stereotyping;
- confuse concepts that really need to be clearer;
- assume certain understandings of culture, ethnicity, religion or diversity.

Teachers might also like to reflect on the kinds of teaching approaches and methodologies used in the examples, by asking questions such as:

- Does this example use the phenomenological, interpretative, dialogical or contextual approach, or a mixture of these?
- To what extent does this example use co-operative learning?
- What place does empathetic communication have in this example?

- In what way does the example employ any kind of distancing or simulation technique?
- What kind of safe space would this example need for its use?
- What forms of dialogue are encouraged or not by this example?
- What images or portrayals of religion or diversity are contained within this example? Are they appropriate?

Particularly important for intercultural education are the questions:

- To what extent does this example promote the tolerance, reciprocity, civic responsibility, reflection and moderation advocated in the earlier sections of this reference book?
- To what extent does this example allow the secular child to have a place and a voice where it is appropriate to the nature of the content?

In cases where the example is felt to lack one or more of these elements, how could the example be modified to include them?

Fifth, there is the question of transferability. At times, it is difficult, and not always productive, to use the practice of another. What works in one context and has come from the mind of one teacher is not easy to replicate in another context and from the mind of a different teacher. It is therefore important to realise that these examples are not offered primarily for direct use. They are offered to stimulate thinking about their transferability. For example, the use of a text in one country is unlikely to be directly useful in another country, but the methodology of using a text is transferable if a similar practice is based on a different text that is more relevant to the new context.

Schools are encouraged, therefore, to ask themselves questions such as:

- Could I use this example in my school? If not, why not?
- Could I use the methodology of this example and adapt it to fit within my own teaching programme? If so, what similar stimulus would I want to use and how could I use it?
- Can I take the basic concept of this example and apply it to my own curriculum programme with different resources, in my own school or community?
- Do I have the kind of resources needed for this practice? If not, how could I get them?

Sixth, the examples all show the importance of clear learning objectives, and then activities that are based on them. Unintended consequences are always possible in education, for education is a dynamic and living encounter between minds. For example, it might be that dealing with a theme which occurs in a number of different religions leads inadvertently to a reductionist approach to those religions and artificially minimises real differences between them. Unless the objectives of the teaching and learning are clear, the activities are unlikely to deal most effectively with the religious diversity and intercultural education. Learning objectives for understanding religious diversity may be very varied. They could include learning about religions in a factual or cognitive way, or learning from religion through critical evaluation. Not all the examples given include both these. Teachers need to be aware of the danger of having too many objectives from the same piece of work or activity. A limited number of learning objectives that are achieved is better than a large number that are not.

Finally, it is important that each activity has its appraisal or evaluation of success. Teachers might like to analyse the examples given to see how the appraisals evaluate the success or otherwise of the example, and how the example might be modified to achieve a better outcome. This approach will enable the examples of current practice included in this reference book to become examples of good practice in other schools across Europe.

Using a text from a novel: Little Shoukri (Cyprus)

Context

This lesson is based on an extract from the novel *It is clouding over* by Menelaos Loundemis, pp. 30-33.[17]

Objectives

Pupils should be able to:

- place the novel in its location and historical context and understand the events behind it;
- empathise with the characters and their feelings;
- understand the real meaning of "exchange of populations";
- realise that ordinary people and especially children can easily develop friendships and love, regardless of race, nationality and religion;
- realise the negative effects of hatred, discrimination and fanaticism on human life and the world;
- become aware of the devastating consequences of wars for ordinary people.

Themes addressed

- Similarities between people from different cultural and religious backgrounds.
- Friendship between ordinary people and children irrespective of differences in nationality, ethnicity or religion.
- Relations between states and the political ends and interests leading to imposed differences.

Target/size of group

A whole class of about 30 pupils aged about 13.

---

17. "Συννεφιαζει" Μ. Λουντμης, Εκδοσεις "Ελλην ικα Γραμματα" Β ΄Εκδοςη Αθηνα 2000 σσ. 30-33.

Persons involved

The teacher, the pupils.

Time needed for preparation and implementation

Two 45-minute sessions for implementation.

Teaching strategies used

Listening, discussion and reflection.

Description of the activity

First lesson

a. Starter activity – images or perceptions of persons of different national-ities, comments on the images, discussion of "Love for our neighbour".

b. A pupil reads the biographical note on the author; another pupil reads an introductory note and commentary.[18]

c. After reading the extract from the novel, there is discussion on the spon-taneous feelings and impressions of the pupils.

d. The teacher asks the pupils to write a summary of the content for homework. Alternatively, the pupils can seek further information about the period of the novel through the internet or books.

Second lesson

e. Pupils identify characteristic phrases from the text that describe the atmosphere/scene of the first lesson.

f. Pupils study and analyse the relationship between the Turkish boy Shoukri and his friend, the author/narrator; they discuss the elements which join or separate them. The great friendship between the two chil-dren, despite their differences, is stressed, but they will be obliged to part. There is analysis of the children's feelings before and after their parting with reference to specific parts of the text.

g. During the lesson the teacher poses questions to make the pupils aware that war was indirectly responsible for Shoukri's death. Such questions are: Why did the children have to separate? What reasons would make the chil-dren live apart? This helps pupils to realise the devastating consequences of war and importance of love for fellow human beings.

---

18. Found in the book on p. 90.

h. Pupils are to discover and discuss the relationship of the extract to current Cypriot and international affairs, with discussion of central and secondary ideas.

i. A piece of homework is set that allows pupils to be creative and develop critical thinking, such as:

- Write a letter to a Turkish Cypriot today, about children wanting to forsake the hatred dividing two peoples and wishing for a united homeland.
- "A Contemporary Shoukri" – state your views on the ideal of friendship between peoples and what must be done regarding Greco-Turkish friendship to open up to us ways for a just and viable solution to the Cyprus problem.
- Complete a table to present the results and consequences on humanity from wars and from peace: war = pain; peace = love.

A comparative study: rites, festivals, practices and places of worship (France)

Context

The conclusion of a history course on "the legacies of antiquity" for a first-year secondary class, or a second-year secondary class in a sequence of lessons on the early days of Islam and the western Christian church, or in a civics education lesson on "the rejection of discrimination". (Depending on the level, some or all of the lesson will be given (in the first-year class, for instance, work may be limited to Judaism and Christianity; in the second-year class, Islam will be compared with Christianity; while civics education will encompass all three religions.) Some, but not all of the documents will be used for another activity on the "festivals and calendars of the mono-theist religions".

Objectives

Pupils should be able to:

- explain the continuation among 21st-century believers of faiths and practices dating from antiquity and the Middle Ages;
- develop tolerance through knowledge and open minds to religious diversity;
- gain an understanding of the interrelationships between the rites, festivals and places of worship of the religions present in France.

Teaching strategies

- Dialogue-based teaching and explanations of photographs and documents.
- Analysis, comparison, study of connections between documents.

Themes

- Three examples of festivals: one Christian, one Jewish, one Muslim.
- Three places of worship: the church, the synagogue, the mosque.
- Three ceremonies: Sunday mass, the Sabbath, Friday prayers.

Target group/group size

- First-year secondary class or second-year secondary class of 25 pupils.

Preparation time needed

- Three hours; lesson preparation is fairly rapid; more time is needed to collect or produce the documents.

Teaching time needed

- One and a half hours.

Description of the activity

Phase 1: explain the purpose of the activity (getting to know the different faiths through their everyday activities, the premises they use and their family festivals).

Phase 2: show pictures on the theme: Christmas meal, Ramadan meal, Passover meal.

- Ask pupils to describe the pictures.
- Give the necessary explanations and information.
- Get pupils to find out about the origins of these festivals.

Phase 3: same exercise with reference to places of worship.

- Study the activities of believers, priests, imams, rabbis.
- Description of premises, their functions, their meaning.

A written outline is gradually recorded, in the form of a full or partial comparative table:

	Christianity	**Judaism**	**Islam**
Ceremonies	Mass	Saturday prayers	Friday prayers
Religious festivals	Christmas Easter	Passover	Eid (the breaking of the fast)
Places	Churches	Synagogues	Mosques

Teaching material and equipment used

- Slides from "La documentation photographique, Le fait religieux en France", No. 8033:

  i. Passover meal in a Sephardic family, Paris region, 1980;

  ii. breaking the fast with a family meal, Paris region, 2001;

  iii. Friday prayers in Evry mosque, 1999;

  iv. prayers in a synagogue.

- Personal slides:
  - i. Christmas meal in a French family
  - ii. Sunday mass in Evry cathedral.

- Photocopies of document describing the three monotheist religions and the meanings of their festivals (see appendix).

- Classroom overhead projector.

Appraisal and evaluation

Activity considered "successful" for having aroused pupils' interest and conveyed to them some items of basic knowledge about religions. It certainly made possible better knowledge of "others".

Appendix

Sample of information supplied by the contributor regarding the religions studied

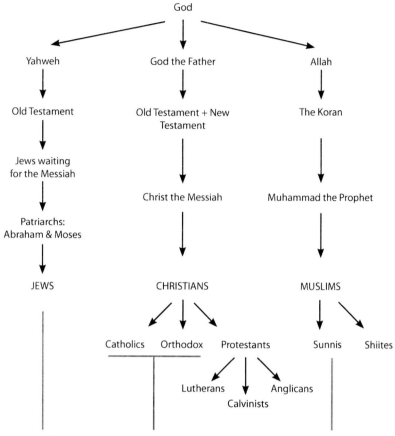

Easter: liberation of the Israelites from slavery in Egypt

Pentecost: giving of the law to Moses

Tisha B'Av: day of mourning for the destruction of the Temple (70)

Feast of Tabernacles

Yom Kippur (day of atonement)

Celebration of the Torah

Festival of Lights

Purim: saving of the Jews of Persia

Lent: 40-day fast corresponding to the period for which Christ fasted in the wilderness

Good Friday: death of Christ on the cross

Easter: resurrection of Christ

Ascension: ascension of Christ into heaven (40 days after Easter)

Pentecost: revelation through the apostles

Assumption: (Catholic) ascension of the Virgin into heaven

Hijra: departure of Muhammad from Mecca to Medina (622)

Night of pardon

Ramadan: fast from sunrise to sunset

Revelation to Muhammad, the Night of Destiny

End of Ramadan: Eid-ul-Fitr

Great Pilgrimage to Mecca (the Hadj)

Festival of Sacrifice (Eid-al-Adha)

Using original sources: dialogue between religions and cultures (Germany)

Context

A multicultural group of pupils studying practical philosophy at the Stiftisches Humanistisches Gymnasium in Mönchengladbach took this as an opportunity for joint discussion of the question whether, at a time when public opinion and the press were focusing on cultural differences, there was any real chance of building together a bridge to the future in a multicultural, multireligious society. The pupils in year 9 belong to a variety of religions and religious communities and also include some who have not been baptised or who describe themselves as atheists. Muslims, Jews, Buddhists, Christians (Protestants and Catholics) are represented, and one boy is a Jehovah's Witness.

Learning objectives

The pupils should be able to:

- gain knowledge of the ethical foundations of the world's main religions;

- experience a practical dialogue with representatives of the main religions concerning their religion's ethical foundations;

- identify similarities and differences in the religions' basic scriptures;

- discuss with local Christian, Muslim, Jewish and Buddhist representatives at the school;

- organise an exhibition in the school presenting the result of the "Bridge to the future" joint project.

Teaching strategies

- Text analysis.
- Live encounters.
- Specialist opinions / panel discussion.
- Classroom discussion.
- In-school exhibition.

Themes addressed

- Diversity and commonality.
- Common values.
- Attempt to find a possible consensus between religions and cultures.
- Practical dialogue – are the theories workable in practice?

Target group/size of group

- Year 9 – 25 pupils.

Partners

- Local representatives of various religions.

Time needed for preparation

- Planning should begin three months before the start of the activity.
- Two weeks to prepare the educational visits – each visit entails three hours' teaching time.
- After each trip at least three hours of lessons must be devoted to the follow-up and the preparation of the next visit.

Time needed for implementation

- Two one-hour lessons per week, for at least eight to nine weeks.

Description of the activity

Stage 1. Diversity or commonality?

Two newspaper photographs served as food for thought in the search for a common foundation – a bridge to the future.

Source: Die ZEIT 14.3.2002 © OL.

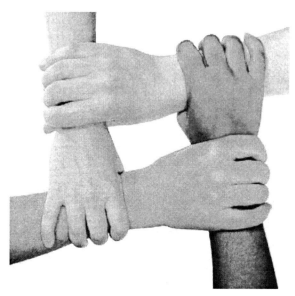

Source: Rheinischer Merkur of 16.1.2003 (photo: RF/Corbes).

Cultural diversity generates anxiety and causes the raising of barriers. The rambler in his walking gear against the mountainous background is a familiar image; the large Muslim family in its traditional costumes is a striking one. The pupils consider that this family simply doesn't fit in with the scenery. The words appearing in the speech balloon illustrate the difference: the rambler ("Wanderer") belongs in his setting, the immigrant ("Einwanderer") is a foreign body. But must this always be the case? The young people interpret the picture as contrasting with the second image – "Unity brings strength" – hands of people from different racial backgrounds form a supporting network. Together, people stand a chance.

Pupils then sought to identify a common foundation, on which a shared bridge to the future could be built:

• Religions have considerable significance in shaping our lives.

• Religions and philosophies will remain sources of wisdom even in the future.

• Knowledge of the riches and diversity of spiritual resources can potentially be destructive, but there is also a constructive potential, which should be turned to use.

Stage 2. Common values

Pupils wanted to find more concrete evidence for the assertion that there are fundamental values common to all religions. Which problems could be solved if, for instance, responsible behaviour vis-à-vis others and the community were to become a general rule of conduct? Recent media reports were examined to see to what extent common principles and mutual responsibilities constituted a central focus of the news coverage. The young people were very disappointed to have to note that such reporting was in the minority. Doubts were expressed about the theory of the existence of common fundamental values. The pupils accordingly wished to ascertain themselves, by consulting the original sources, whether such values existed and could serve as a basis for dialogue between cultures and religions.

Stage 3. The search for a possible consensus between religions and cultures

Excepts from the Old Testament, the New Testament and the Koran were interpreted as such and situated in their historical context. When analysing the texts the doubts experienced by the young people in the earlier stages of the teaching project were taken seriously. The working papers on the basic scriptures were structured in such a way that the pupils had room to express their own thoughts.

Live encounters with representatives of the major religions (visits to the Minster, the mosque, the synagogue and the Buddhist temple) provided the pupils with additional guidance.

It was then asked whether the different systems of values included a common fundamental idea. Humanity was identified as a value common to all religions and philosophies. It was then a matter of tracing fresh examples of this value in the messages of the world religions and philosophies.

Stage 4. Practical dialogue – are the theories workable in practice?

Identifying a consensus in the basic religious and philosophical writings is the first step, initiating a dialogue in order to transform the theoretical knowledge into a practical form of co-operation (and not just co-existence) is the necessary second step.

If common basic convictions can be identified, why do people not deal with each other according to those fundamental principles? Pupils wished to verify whether the common principles they had uncovered were workable in practice.

Representatives of various religions (Christians, Muslims, Jews and Buddhists) were invited to the school to participate in a panel debate on the theme: "Is there a common foundation – a bridge to the future, which people of all cultures and religions can take?" The panel discussion confirmed the results of the young people's learning experience. They then identified the central question to be addressed in the subsequent lessons: Can the basic consensus be applied not just in minor but also in major matters, and accordingly in a political context?

Stage 5. Summary

The pupils agreed that joint discussion of the different religions' fundamental values could form a basis for peaceful co-existence in a multicultural society.

A small exhibition was mounted to present the project's results to the other pupils in the school. The young people did not take a negative view of the fact that in the course of the lessons many questions remained unanswered and the approaches to numerous problems had to be restricted in order to keep within the boundaries of the chosen theme. They rather expressed the wish to take the unanswered questions as a starting point for an in-depth debate on the theme of human rights during their coming lessons.

Appendix

1. Text: Judaism; Exodus 20, 1–21   2. Text: Christianity; Matthew 5–7   3. Text: Islam; Koran, Sura 17
The golden rule of humanity   Source: citation from Hans Küng: "A global ethic for global politics and economics", Munich, Piper, 1997, p. 140.   *Confucius* (ca. 551-489 BC): "What you do not want done to yourself, do not do to others" (Analects, 15, 23).   *Rabbi Hillel* (60 BC-10 AD): "What is hateful to you, do not do to anyone else" (Sabbath 31a).   *Jesus of Nazareth*: "Whatsoever you should wish that man should do to you, do you also to them" (Matthew 7, 12; Luke 6, 31).   *Islam:* "Not one of you is a believer until he loves for his brother what he loves for himself" (40 Hadith of an-Nawawi 13).   *Buddhism*: "For a state that is not pleasant or delightful to me must also be to him also; and a state that is not pleasing or delightful to me, how could I inflict that upon another?" (Samyutta Nikaya V, 535.53-354.2).   *Hinduism*: "One should not behave towards others in a way which is disagreeable to oneself. This is the essence of morality" (Mahabharata XIII.114.8).
Immanuel Kant: three formulations of the categorical imperative: 1. "So act as if you were through your maxims a law-making member of a kingdom of ends."   2. "Act as if the maxim of your action was to become through your will a universal law of nature."   3. "Act in such a way that you always treat humanity, whether in your own person or in the person of any other, never simply as a means, but at the same time as an end."

Use of an artefact: the oil lamp (Greece)

Context

A lesson from an intercultural junior High school in Athens, where the pupils are of Orthodox Christian and Muslim backgrounds.

Objectives

Pupils should be able to become aware of the significance of the oil lamp in the three religions: Judaism, Christianity and Islam.

Teaching strategies

Question and answer, discussion, searching and finding, role play, artwork in decoration, use of literature and writing.

Partners

The Synagogue of Patras, which pupils visited for this activity.

Themes addressed

Differences and similarities between people from different cultural and religious backgrounds.

Target group/size of group

A whole class of about 23 pupils, aged between 10 and 12.

Persons involved

The teacher, the museum education officer.

Time needed for preparation and implementation

One hour for preparation and about one hour for implementation.

Description of visit

The visit to the synagogue began with a discussion with the pupils on the use of the Holy Oil Lamp as the "eternal light" in the synagogue, where it always burns during services, and certain holidays and in memory of the souls of the departed. Then at the Jewish Holidays display case, there was another discussion on the presence and the use of the oil lamp in Jewish homes, focusing on the lighting of the holy light to usher in the holy Sabbath Day. The children sat down in front of the display case. The museum educator invited them to recount their own and their families' experiences concerning the significance of the use of the holy lamp at the home, in the place of prayer, in religion and in tradition. Their accounts referred the lighting of the oil lamp before the Christian home icon stand, as well as its use in memory of the dead in the Muslim religion. A brief recording of what the children had said led to the conclusion that the uses of the oil lamp in the main three monotheist religions were similar or even identical. The children also noticed that in all three religions the same materials were used to light the oil lamp; olive oil, a little water and a wick. Then the children busied themselves with a creative activity; they decorated a glass oil lamp with fresh cut flowers as we do customarily in the Romaniot Jewish Community of Ioannina before the celebration of Yom Kippur (the Day of Atonement). Finally, before the evaluation of the programme, the museum educator handed the children photographs of the oil lamps among the Museum's exhibits. She suggested that they should continue work in class by searching for poems, songs, fairy tales and stories that make mention of the oil lamp, and by making a written record of relevant family accounts.

Description of the activity

- Getting acquainted – welcome to the museum, self-adhesive labels to display pupils' names.

- Asking pupils to talk about what they think they can do here and what not.

- Introduction to surroundings: have you been here before? What did you see? What did you like/not like? Have you been to other museums? Which? What did you like/not like?

- Introduction to subject: brainstorming on the oil lamp. Describe its use at home, church, synagogue and mosque, drawing out common features and differences. Refer to materials in making the lamps in all three religions, with their decorative symbols and motifs.

- Search and find: search the museum, find lamps and information about them. How are they used, in synagogue, home, during celebrations, in the journey through life to death, and related customs?

- Presentation: the pupils present the information they have gathered on the use of the oil lamp in Judaism. There follows a discussion on its use in the Christian and Muslim religions.
- Creative activities: role play – the pupils role play the lighting of the lamp in celebration of the Kabalat Shabbat (ushering in the Sabbath); decoration – the pupils decorate an oil lamp for celebrating Yom Kippur (Day of Atonement).
- Evaluation: the pupils were asked what new things they had seen and learnt at the museum today. What would you like to learn about next time you visit the museum?
- Further work that may be set by teachers: the pupils could find passages in literature, folk songs, poems and fairy tales that mention oil lamps; they could also make a written record of family accounts of the use of the oil lamp.

Teaching/pedagogical materials and equipment used

Paper, drawing implements, photographs of lamps, fresh cut flowers.

Appraisal

The activity was very productive and was used several times because it was so successful.

Organising a cultural exchange: Rome – Tel Aviv (Holy See)

Context

An exchange between the Santa Maria Degli Angeli Institute (upper secondary school) in Rome and Kalay High School, Giv'ataim – Tel Aviv.

Learning objectives

To provide direct, meaningful experience of dialogue between young people in order to lay the foundations for mutual respect and understanding.

To embed a culture of peace in everyday life.

To develop knowledge and understanding of the culture of young Israelis and young Italian Christians.

Preparation and teaching strategies

- Preparatory classes with preparation of written texts and presentations; introductory exchange of emails between pupils participating in the scheme; photographic exhibitions.
- Setting up of working groups, daily presentations (prepared in advance) followed by time for asking questions and sharing impressions and experiences.
- Meetings with the officials who backed the project with experts involved in promoting inter-faith dialogue.
- Evening activities: for example, five-a-side football match.
- Guided tours and visits.
- Participation in Hanukkah and Shabbat celebrations.

Themes addressed

- Life of a young person in Israel/Italy today (with special emphasis on dealing with conflict situations – compulsory military service/conscientious objection).
- Being descendants of families who personally experienced the Holocaust.
- Being Jewish (identity traditions) / being Jewish in Israel.

- Being Christian / non-practising Christian.
- The international news media.

Number of participants in the group

Approximately 20, aged between 16 and 18.

Time needed for preparation

Many months of planning, and many weeks of organisation.

Time needed for implementation

One week of activities at the school, with many hours per day for the staff.

Material and equipment required

Texts, internet research facilities, written and multimedia material, space.

Description of activity

Day 1:   Arrive, welcome, meal, acclimatisation visit, evening entertainment.

Days 2-6: Visit to the different classes, meals, relaxation, external visits, entertainment, seminars.

Day 7:   Evaluations, farewells, travel home.

Appraisal

The experience helped to improve the pupils' interpersonal skills and to make them more accepting of people different from themselves. There was opportunity to step outside their everyday environment and to transcend prejudice. The exchange served to broaden the pupils' mental horizons and to make them more curious about the geography and culture of other countries. The activity was initially regarded with some trepidation by pupils and their families yet in the event, it proved to be an exciting experience, both intellectually and emotionally speaking. New relationships were formed, some of which have proved lasting.

Language could be a problem. Next time, more time should be set aside for unscheduled discussion.

Organising a whole school event: International Week (Norway)

Context

This programme of activities comes from a rural but multicultural district of Norway. More than 40 nationalities and four main religions are represented in this junior school, which likes to think of itself as a "world in miniature". Multicultural links have almost become a "brand" of the school. It is important to see the programme over a seven-year perspective, from year 1 to year 7.

General objectives

- To focus on what is common for all cultures.

- To emphasise and show cultural aspects of two-cultural families and teachers' use of mother tongue.

- To strengthen the multicultural environment of the school and families' relationships to it and the local community.

- Increase multicultural awareness and pride in home cultures.

- Affirm position of teachers of mother languages and help them become known.

- Increase sense of unity among the children.

- Enrich all our lives by sharing and performing aspects of different cultures.

Specific to multicultural play (year 1)

- Learn about each other by playing games and singing songs from the various countries we come from.

Specific to national costumes (year 2)

- See and draw them.

Specific to drama activities (year 2)

- Dramatise the "same" fairy tale in the way it is told in the different cultures.

Specific to games (indoor and outdoor) (year 3)

- Learn to play new games.

Specific to fairy tales (year 4)

- Read and perform different fairy tales from different countries.

Specific to children's rights

- Learn about children's rights.

Specific to international dancing (year 5)

- Learn dances from different countries.

Specific to art – illustrating a story (year 5)

- Listen to the ballet suite by Igor Stravinsky, King Kastsjeis dance from "The Firebird".
- Listen to the story of the Firebird and make appropriate illustrations.

Specific to international food (year 6)

- Learn to make dishes from different countries.

Specific to human rights (year 6)

- Learn about some human rights.

Specific to United Nations (year 7)

- Learn about the origin of the UN.

Specific to work of peace (year 7)

- Find out about peacemakers.

Specific to anti-racism (year 7)

- Find out about work against racism in Norway and other places.

Description of activities

Start the week with an assembly, with children in national costumes joining a parade, and singing the school song as well as other songs. During the week have an international evening when families come to school with traditional food from their home countries, and children perform for their parents. Finish with a closing ceremony, with a performance and invited guests. During the week there is a good deal of group work, with role plays, singing and dancing, story telling, cultural films, project work, use of the internet and formal teaching. When Ramadan does not coincide with 24 October, United Nations Day, it is also celebrated, with representatives from the local Evangelical Church, a Mosque and the Human Ethical Organisation, all speaking about human rights in light of their religious or secular standpoint.

Partnership

- Teachers of the mother tongues have a central role. The school coordinator for multicultural activities organises the week with a schedule of activities etc. Teachers vary in their work but try to contribute to the topic in their form teaching.
- Parents join in the telling and showing of things from their countries such as food making, dancing and singing.
- Other local and international entertainers often perform at the opening and closing ceremonies.
- A multicultural school committee, with representatives from the local church and mosque as well as teachers, plays an important part.

Themes addressed

- Cultural aspects of the many countries represented in the school.
- Knowledge, respect and tolerance of different cultures.
- United Nations Day, 24 October (see below).

Target group/size of group

Whole classes aged between 6 and 12.

Time needed for preparation and implementation

The week involves the whole school, so preparation in advance is necessary. Preparation of class activities with different topics is variable, though lessons should be prepared several weeks ahead of use. Making a school song is very important, as it is used not just in the week but also throughout the year.

Teaching/pedagogical materials and equipment used

- The school song

> We come from Lommedalen, Baghdad and Drammen, Pakistan, Karasjokk and the US!
>
> We bring along language and lots of dialects;
> we understand each other well!
>
> We speak Kurd and "drammenser" here. We talk Urdu, Arabic and German!
>
> But we are Rykkinn-people, and we are just as good, no matter where we originate!
>
> We come from Senegal, Skui and Kabul, Denmark, Somalia and Kurdistan!
>
> We bring our music, songs and dancing, and we see that it is possible to live in harmony!
>
> We play tabla, djembe and sitar here. We dance zorba, polka and reel!
>
> Father Jacob we sing in many tongues, we sing it our way!
>
> We come from Tromso, Paris and Morocco, Kosovo, Lebanon, Nesby'n and Kjerr!
>
> The food we like can be different, but most of it we can get here.
>
> We like couscous – mild or hot! We smell of garlic, chilli, fish and "Klubb"
> Most of it tastes nice!
>
> We come from Haugesund and Palestine, from the Philippines, Drobakk and Ski!
>
> Our ideas can be different, but our thoughts are free!
>
> We celebrate Christmas, Easter and 8 March. We celebrate Id and Ramadan.
>
> But on 17 May together we march, to celebrate all that we can.
>
> We left closed down farms and factories; we left famines, wars and storms.
>
> Here we found work, safety and sunshine; here we live well!
>
> We play football, drums and tennis here; we join youth clubs and go skiing.
>
> We are Gommerud kids, and we are just as good, no matter where we originate!

- Songs like Brother James (or John) in different languages, Frère Jacques, Fader Jacob, Waaryaa Jaamac, Baba Jacob, Pater Jakob, Voae Jakob, Bab Yakob, Panie Janie.

- Different games, for example roofball, pairs, colour game, fire-fire; we have blowing competitions.

- Flags from different countries.
- Sports equipment.

Appraisal

- The week is the climax of the whole year, and is looked forward to by children at the school, parents, older children who have left, and is really enjoyed by all. It is easier as we collect ideas from previous years and have more to draw on each time.
- The enthusiasm of the parents when contributing with lots of delicious food from all corners of the world on our international evening makes a real difference to the evening and increases the anticipation of the children.
- Some of the parents who don't normally join in social meetings at the school throughout the school year find that the international evening is well worth supporting.
- Co-operation with the teachers of the mother tongues really contributes to a more varied cultural diversity. These teachers are very important for the pupils during this week, because they secure a more central role for all children in the school.
- The fact that we organise this week every year contributes to a multicultural identity for ethnic Norwegian children as well as children with other cultural backgrounds; differences become an enriching strength.
- Avoid the days of Ramadan when organising the intercultural week.

> Some examples of how enriching can be seen in the questions for discussions amongst the older pupils, enabling them to learn more about each other:
> - Can Muslims or children from other religions go to the local church?
> - What's the difference between taking part in a service and joining in when visiting an old church with its history and symbols?
> - Can Muslims join in on a Pilgrim-walk through our local community, following in the footsteps of our forefathers?
> - Can Muslims have girlfriends and boyfriends?
> - Can Muslim boys have girlfriends, while the girls can't have boyfriends?
> - Are Norwegian girls "whores" because they dress in clothes showing their bare stomach and have boyfriends?
> - Do Norwegian girls deserve as much respect as Muslim girls?
> - Is it necessary to wear a "hijab" to be a good Muslim?
> - Must other people concern themselves about somebody wearing a hijab?

- Everybody who wants to wear his or her hijab in the classroom can, but nobody can wear a cap. Is that fair or unfair?
- Is it better to be a Muslim than a Christian or vice versa?
- Is it possible not to believe in anything?
- Are those who don't celebrate Christmas to be pitied?
- Are those who fast to be pitied?
- Al Qaeda is an Islamic organisation. Are all Muslims members or supporters?
- Must all Muslims support holy war?
- Are Muslims to blame for 9/11?
- Are God and Allah two different gods, or are they the same?

Example: United Nations Day

24 October: United Nations Day gathering in the hall

In the spring of 2004 the school invited interested representatives from the local mosque, the local congregation, the Human Ethical Organisation, and the organisation of parents and teachers to a multicultural meeting on "Values". The aim was to work out common values for the school and the groups mentioned. The school emphasised the importance of grown-ups showing each other respect and standing up for some of the same important values between humans. The meeting was most successful, with the church and the mosque expressing a desire for a better and closer relationship. All representatives emphasised the role the UN and Human Rights play. With this in mind, the school invited the representatives from a mosque, an Evangelical church and the Human Ethical Organisation to join in an assembly on 24 October and afterwards to visit some of the classes. The representatives were invited to express their views as to why and how they would celebrate UN Day and human rights in accordance with their religion. The children had the opportunity to ask questions like:

- Is there just one God, many Gods or no God? Are God and Allah the same?
- Is it appropriate for a Muslim to go to church or, vice versa, for a Lutheran to go to a mosque?
- Is it better to be a Christian than a Muslim or vice versa?
- Why do you fast? Is it difficult to fast?

The former bishop of Oslo, Gunnar Staalseth, was invited to our school because he has played an active part in developing good relations between different religious leaders in Norway and Europe. In addition he has also been very active in work against racism. He visited the year 6 and 7 children.

He told them about his work with different religious leaders and their mutual work for peace, especially after 9/11.

He spoke about his visits to India and was asked about his attitude towards Indian religious leaders and their religion, Hinduism. He expressed a deep respect for the way the Hindus take care of all living creatures. He also told the pupils about Mahatma Ghandi and his struggle for peace and justice in a non-violent way.

He told them a lot about his work here in Norway. This led to a lot of questions from the children, such as:

- How does a bishop live? Do you have a family and friends?
- How is a bishop dressed in church? (He was wearing a clergy shirt with a normal suit.)
- What was it like to marry the Norwegian Crown Prince and his wife and baptise their children?

Out of school visits: places of religious worship and organisations offering an alternative outlook on life (Norway)

Context

This programme of activities comes from a rural but multicultural district of Norway. More than 40 nationalities and four main religions are represented in this junior school, which likes to think of itself as a "world in miniature". Multicultural links have almost become a "brand" of the school. It is important to see the programme over a six-year perspective, from year 2 to year 7.

General objectives

- To become acquainted with other world religions and outlooks for moral standards and interpretation of life.
- Promote an understanding, respect and capacity for dialogue between human beings with different views on questions of belief.

Specific for visit to local mosque (years 2 and 3)

- Develop capacity for respect and tolerance towards other pupils.
- See and hear Muslim classmates at the Qur'an school.

Specific for visit to local Lutheran (Protestant) church (year 4)

- Get acquainted with its history and symbols.

Specific for visit to Franciscan monastery or Catholic church (year 4)

- Get acquainted with life of St Francis of Assisi and his successors.
- Get acquainted with its history and symbols.

Specific for visit to 'Blue Mosque' in Oslo (year 5)

- Get acquainted with its history, architecture, symbols and Muslim beliefs.

Specific for visit to 'House of Humanities' in Oslo (year 6)

- Get acquainted with its organisation (Human-Ethical Association).

- Get to know about humanistic ethical ceremonies, atheism and agnosticism.

Specific for visit to synagogue in Oslo (year 6)
- Get acquainted with its history, symbols and beliefs.

Specific for visit to Buddhist Centre in Oslo (year 7)
- Get acquainted with its history, architecture, symbols and beliefs.

Specific for visit to Hindu temple (year 7)
- Get acquainted with its history, symbols and beliefs.

Planning and teaching strategies

Before each visit, read about relevant topics and discuss relevant conventions and customs so pupils are prepared. How to behave in places of worship is always covered, as is discussion on how to show respect and tolerance. It is also important to deal with any nervousness or fears of the children (for example seeing Christ hanging on a cross, or visiting an area with graves).

- After the visit to the local mosque, making comparisons between what is said in the Bible and the Qur'an about the birth of Jesus.
- Role-plays at Christmas, with checks on what is suitable for pupils of different faiths to read, sing or do – contacting parents where necessary.
- Follow-up work where children record their impressions from the visits, with appropriate drawings, and then share them.
- Marking the celebrations of not just Christmas but also Id (end of Muslim fast during Ramadan) at appropriate times of the year; developing an Id song and a role-play for this purpose (see below).

Partnership

The school also has a co-ordinator for multicultural activities who has organised a list of places to visit with phone numbers. The teachers of each form work in partnership with the officials at the various places visited. When visiting the local mosque, we co-operate with parents of Muslim children in the class. The local evangelical church has also worked out a programme which functions well for children of different cultural backgrounds. The programme of the local church is such that the parents of children from other religions find it acceptable for their children to join in.

Themes addressed

- Differences and similarities between people from different cultural and religious backgrounds, mostly represented in the school.
- Respect and tolerance for such people.

Target group/size of group

- Whole classes aged between 7 and 12.

Time needed for preparation and implementation

- Organising the visits by telephone well in advance is necessary (three months).
- Preparation of class activities with different topics is variable, though lessons should be prepared several weeks ahead of use.
- Each visit normally takes one day, but follow-up activities will vary in length.

Teaching/pedagogical materials and equipment used

- Symbols of different religions brought to school by the children.
- Paper, drawing implements, etc. for recording and follow-up work.

The Id song

Wa Marhaba bika	Ja, Ramadan; Velkommen til deg	Ja, Ramadan
Welcome to you	Yes, Ramadan; Ja shahra gufrani	Ja, Ramadan
Gledens maaned	Ja, Ramadan; Tilgivelsenes maaned	Ja, Ramadan
The month of happiness Yes, Ramadan		

A Ramadan role-play formed as a dialogue between Muslim children and their Norwegian friends giving explanations about the fasting period.

Appraisal

- Children familiar with a place of worship already, or who have a place of worship, find similarities and differences easy to realise. They find it interesting to see what other places are like and develop a more relaxed attitude towards other cultures than their own. Those who belong to a place of worship take a pride in showing and telling others about it.
- All parents are advised to let their children come on the visits, since there is no question of the children practising the religion of the place visited. It is to give information and understanding only. Parents have developed a very positive attitude towards this programme.

- All places of worship have been very forthcoming. The children, with all their questions and comments, have been taken seriously. This develops a good and relaxed relationship based on tolerance and respect for each other.

- A visit to a place of worship gives a different type of knowledge, an experience, that can't be compared to the school presentations. It seems to create an openness and relaxed attitude towards differences in religious and cultural backgrounds. Good dialogue takes place between the children and members of the faith whose building they visit. See below for two examples of dialogue that took place.

- The children learn how to enter a place of worship with a quiet anticipation and good behaviour. They experience that they find the same peaceful atmosphere whatever place of worship they visit.

- We have seen that pupils who were once nervous or afraid about visiting the Church or the local burial ground have become relaxed about visits since they have experienced that there is nothing to be afraid of. This has been obtained through more knowledge about a once-foreign culture.

- We have come to realise that through this programme we create a ground for taking seriously both one's own and others' religious or secular outlook on life.

- The children, already familiar with a particular place of worship, feel pride in showing their place of worship. It is a very concrete way for the school to show interest and pay attention to the backgrounds of many pupils.

- The children kept up a keen interest throughout the visit, thanks to a very forthcoming and keenly interested "guide", a member of the church who has specifically taken on the task of sharing with schoolchildren the Catholic faith and traditions.

Example of dialogues when visiting the "Blue" mosque in Oslo

When entering the mosque, the imam showed us where we could leave our things and where to put our shoes before entering the prayer room. We all sat down on the carpeted floor. The imam said he would tell us about the five main rules in the life of a Muslim, "the five columns", and that the children could ask questions from time to time. First of all the pupils were very interested in the beautifully patterned prayer room. Amongst the patterns they spotted something in writing:

P(upil): What is that written on the wall?

I(mam): It is "Allah", written in Arabic letters. In Islam we are not allowed to make pictures of Allah; instead we decorate with patterns. Allah is the one and only God, and we believe he is the same God that Christians and Jews believe in. A good Muslim reads his creed every day: "There is no God but Allah, and Muhammad is his last prophet." The creed is the first of the five columns.

P: Why do you have seven clocks on the wall?

I: Five of the clocks show the five daily prayer times, the sixth clock shows the time of the Friday prayer and the seventh clock is a "normal" clock, always showing the right time.

P: Why do you pray so many times every day?

I: Because Allah, Himself, told our prophet, Muhammad, to do so. And when we pray, we always turn towards Mecca because we turn towards Allah's house, Ka'bah, built by Ibrahim, allocated in Mecca. Prayer is the second of the five columns.

P: How do you know where Mecca is?

I: Look here! In the prayer room we have built this alcove to show the direction. We always kneel with our bodies pointing towards the alcove. Before we enter the prayer room we wash our face, hands and feet and take a little bit of water through our hair so that we are clean when turning to Allah.

P: But how do you know where Mecca is if you're not in this prayer room?

I: Then we use a so-called "compass of prayer" showing the direction.

P: Why do you believe in Paradise and Hell?

I: Muhammad has said that those who believe in Allah and act according to his commands will go to Paradise. Those who act against his commands will go to Hell. We don't know who will come to Hell. In Hell there are lots of flames as well as very cold, foul drinks, snakes and spiders etc. and those who come there will be punished for what they have done in this life on Earth.

P: Do evil human beings come to Paradise?

I: If you believe in Allah, you come to Paradise.

I: If you kill a person, you go to Hell first, but if you believe in Allah you will be sent to Paradise after having been punished in Hell.

Let me tell you a little anecdote: An old lady met Muhammad. She asked him if old ladies come to Paradise. He told her just young people do so. The old lady started to cry. Then Muhammad comforted her and said you become young again when you arrive in Paradise.

P: Why do you fast?

I: We fast to remind us of how it is to be poor and hungry and thirsty. We don't eat and drink between sunrise and sunset. Instead we think about Allah and the possibilities of doing good deeds.

P: Should children fast?

I: Children don't need to fast and we don't recommend that children going to school fast. Many children wish to do so because the rest of the family do so, but they don't have to. They can wait till they're about 13 or 14 years old, but there is no set rule for when you can start fasting. Those who fast must be strong enough to be without food and drink for so many hours. Also elderly and sick people shouldn't fast.

P: What happens if a person eats or drinks during the fasting hours?

I: Then the person must fast an extra 60 days or give food to poor people. The fasting month in Islam is called Ramadan. Ramadan appears at different times every year, because the Muslim year is 11 days shorter than the year in the westerly world. The Muslim year follows the moon year and not the sun year.

I: Let me tell you something else about the Muslim calendar. Year zero started in the year 622 AD, the year when Muhammad fled from Mecca to Medina. So the year 2005 AD equals 1425-26 in the Muslim calendar.

At the end of Ramadan we give money to the poor people and when Ramadan is finished, we celebrate with a lot of nice food and give each other gifts.

P: Please, tell us about the holy Ka'bah.

I: The Ka'bah stone is placed in Mecca. A black stone has been fastened to the wall of the Ka'bah building. This stone is holy and a good Muslim should try to visit Mecca at least once during his lifetime if he can afford it physically, financially or politically (being allowed a visa). The Ka'bah used to be a building where people worshipped many small gods, but Muhammad was told from Allah that he should clean out the place and only Allah should be worshipped. Each year there is a particular month of pilgrimage and millions of Muslims from all over the world come to praise Allah and kiss the holy black stone in the Ka'bah. The pilgrimage is the fifth column.

The fourth column represents giving to the poor. Muslims pay a tax, a sort of welfare tax, to help the poor. Here in Norway we pay approximately 2.5% of our income, that is 25 crowns out of a thousand crowns.

The pupils asked these and many more questions. He told us that he was very impressed by the children's eagerness to inquire, and the children really enjoyed the opportunity to ask and learn more about the things that they had heard and read about in their book of religious theory at school.

Example of dialogues when visiting St. Halvard's church, a Roman Catholic church in Oslo

P(upil): How come the church looks circular in here but from the outside it looks square?

G(uide): The circular shape points towards something eternal, without a beginning and an end; our eternal Father in Heaven, God, the church service and prayer. The fact that the building looks square on the outside points to the more worldly life with offices, toilets, congregation hall and a monastery on the first floor.

P: Why does it look as if the roof is falling down on us?

G: This church building is very special in the fact that it has got a round dome with the dome pointing downwards. To my knowledge no other church is built in such a way. The architect wanted this architecture to symbolise that God is coming to us, whilst a dome pointing upwards symbolises that the humans are stretching towards God.

P: Why are there holes in the brick wall?

G: It has an acoustic effect. If the walls had been all solid, there would have been an enormous echo.

P: Why are there all these stone pictures in the wall?

G: This series of pictures is called a frieze showing episodes in the life of the holy Francis of Assisi living in Italy 800 years ago. In our church we have a copy of the cross from the church of San Damiano, to remind us of how Francis got his calling. Since Francis died, he has always had successors named after him, the Franciscan monks. Here in our church we have four monks, functioning as priests. We have a very big congregation spread over a vast area.

P: How many belong to your church?

G: About 7,000. It's a good thing everybody doesn't come at the same time, because we couldn't receive them all. But sometimes we borrow Lutheran churches, to give services closer to where parts of our congregation live. And every Palm Sunday we have an ecumenical service together with a Lutheran church. The first part of the service is in their church, and then we walk together to our church to end the service here. The two priests co-operate and both take part in each other's services. Both their church and our church are Christian churches even though there are differences in what we emphasise in our religion.

P: We have heard at school that monks can't marry. Why?

G: That's quite right! Monks and priests choose to live in celibacy so they can spend all their time on other human beings, not having to share their valuable time with family members as well.

G: Now I would like to show you the altar. As you can see it is a square altar on a circular platform, symbolising the relationship between God and the world. Here you can see a little niche with a stone covering it. Inside there is sand and a couple of lockets. The lockets contain relics, that is, little bits of hair, bones or skin from saints in the Catholic Church.

P: How do you become a saint?

G: People who have done a lot of good things sometimes are made holy after they are dead. Very often they were martyrs who were killed for their faith. It has been legal and an old tradition to take parts of their body to different Catholic churches. All our churches in different countries have relics from saints.

P: Why do you have relics?

G: Because we want to show that we are a part of a long succession of human beings.

G: Now I would like to take you to a little side chapel with a statue of our Holy Mother Mary. She is the foremost of all the saints in our church, because she was the mother of Jesus Christ. Nobody else has had such close contact with the Son of God as his mother. We don't praise Mother Mary in the same way as God, but we ask her to pray for us in front of God. We can pray directly to God, but somehow we often prefer Mother Mary to intercede for us.

P: Why do you have that cupboard on top of the altar?

G: We call it the Tabernacle. I'm sure you have heard about the tent that Moses and his people brought with them through the desert. They kept the book rolls with the history of Israel there, so that the sun shouldn't damage them. We keep our oblates, a sort of special bread, there. We eat it in memory of Christ, our Saviour.

Using the arts: intercultural music (Slovenia)

Context

These sessions are based on contemporary Buddhist and Islamic music, and Hinduism: the western jazz tradition and Indian classical music. For further details see the appendix.

They take place in the context of non-confessional education about religions and intercultural education in public elementary schools in Slovenia. They were introductory to themes on Islam and Buddhism, and Hinduism according to the syllabus. This way of introducing the themes through the diversity of music is a "soft approach", using diversity not as a problem but as enrichment.

Objectives

- Promoting intercultural and inter-religious understanding and dialogue through music.
- Improving knowledge and understanding of another's religion and culture.
- Familiarisation with other sources of knowledge.
- Generation of curiosity about and empathy with the culture and religion of others.
- Respecting human dignity and human rights to help learn to live together.

Teaching strategies

- Interactive learning with listening, discussion, explanation, looking at pictures and texts and reflection.

Themes addressed

- Music as a mirror of multicultural reality.
- Differences and similarities between music from different cultural and religious backgrounds.
- Dialogue and friendship between people through music.

Target group/size of group

- A whole class of about 30 pupils (or smaller groups) aged about 13-14.

Persons involved

- The music teacher, the ICT teacher, the pupils.

Time needed for preparation and implementation

- Eight hours' preparation by the teacher to create the presentation of sound and pictures.
- Two hours for implementation.

Description of the activity

- This activity takes place in the ICT classroom.
- The first part is a general introduction to the themes, followed by visual presentation of the material and listening to the music with explanations.

Teaching/pedagogical materials and equipment used

IC technology – computer, LCD projector, multimedia speakers, PowerPoint presentation and CDs (see appendix).

Appraisal

Students reacted enthusiastically. At first the music was a cultural shock, especially the Buddhist chants and the unusual sounds of Nursrat Fateh Ali Khan. But after this initial reaction, the students adjusted from their surprise and did not want to stop listening. After the first hearing of the Qawwali music they started to dance, and were given a task to prepare a choreography for class presentation following the wise saying of an old man "Without experience no knowledge".

APPENDIX (based on information from the CD covers)

Buddhist chants: the basis of traditional Buddhist music is the ritual incantation and instrumentation of the temple. Typically in the case of the Chinese form the meditative sounds themselves reflect man's proximity to nature: flute evoking the wind through trees, wooden drums sound out nature's thunder, hand bells mimicking the flow of water. Chanting helps to concentrate the mind for the participant, but also serves to provide a beautiful almost primal allure for the listener.

Islam Qawwali: the devotional music of the Sufis, as an example of intercultural collaboration, with musicians from different cultures – Canadian, Pakistani, West Indian; the instruments from different continents: the big Brazilian drum, the surdu, the Senegalese djembe, Indian tabla plus harmonium, bass, infinite guitar and keyboards.

Hinduism – Western Jazz Tradition meets Indian Classical Music: in Sanskrit, Shakti literally means energy, or rather, the feminine version of divine energy.

Using language: Arabic Language and Moroccan Culture Education Programme (Spain)

Context

In 1980, the Spanish and Moroccan governments signed a cultural co-operation agreement setting out the basic principles of the Arabic Language and Moroccan Culture Education Programme, which is designed for Moroccan pupils attending Spanish primary and secondary schools. The main areas of co-operation and implementation of the Programme include:

*   Spain facilitates the teaching of Arabic language and Moroccan culture to Moroccan pupils attending Spanish primary and secondary schools.

*   Spanish authorities provide the Moroccan teachers responsible for providing this instruction with the necessary premises, subject to the approval of the governing bodies of the schools concerned.

*   Morocco provides the necessary teaching staff and is fully responsible for them.

*   Spain participates in staff training and in the preparation of teaching material to support the lessons.

The Centre for Educational Research and Documentation (CIDE) co-ordinates the Programme, which was introduced in Spain in 1994/95.

General objectives of the Programme

*   To provide Moroccan pupils with instruction that will help them to preserve their identity, to experience their own culture whilst respecting that of the host country and to develop confidence in themselves and their future.

*   To successfully adapt to school and a new life by fostering tolerance and a sense of community.

Cultural and intercultural objectives

*   To understand the main aspects and features of the social, cultural and political system in their own country and in the Arab world.

- To celebrate the defining features of their culture as a basis for developing an interest in, and respecting, the various aspects of the host-country culture.
- To identify and acknowledge similarities between the cultural values of the Spanish and Moroccan peoples, and the contribution that Arab culture has made to Spanish culture.
- To help pupils of different nationalities and from different cultural backgrounds to participate in exchange activities that promote mutual understanding and respect.
- To foster tolerance, respect and a sense of community.
- To make pupils more aware of the wide range of values and lifestyles found in their own culture and to generate interest in the host-country culture.
- To discourage pupils from discriminating on grounds of race, gender, culture, religion.

Teaching-learning strategies and material

- Audiovisual material, slides, tourism brochures on Morocco, Spain and other countries.
- Highlighting the diversity of the country of origin and the host country.
- Use of situations and events that are close to the pupil and also information gleaned from the media.
- Documents that chart the history of the societies and countries concerned.
- Encouraging the pupils to be active and creative participants in the learning process, with the emphasis on their own experiences, and discussion-based learning.
- Making lessons meaningful by empowering the pupil.
- Teaching them about equality, without making distinctions of any kind or imposing conditions, in an atmosphere of respect, tolerance and fellowship.
- Developing the pupils' sense of identity and self-esteem, by allowing them to design and play their own games, for example.

Themes addressed at different levels

At preparatory level, the cultural and intercultural content is combined, as far as possible, with linguistic content and rooted in the pupils' surrounding environment and personal experience. Later on, it is gradually extended to include broader, more complex concepts. At every level, the work is centred on areas of interest appropriate to the pupils' age and characteristics. The cultural content is made up of various elements: geography, history, art, civic and religious education, covering both Moroccan and Spanish life.

Practical arrangements

Scheme A: designed for schools which have only a small number of Moroccan pupils.

Scheme B: designed for schools which have a large number of Moroccan pupils.

Appraisal

According to information received, the outcome has been positive and encouraging, with the pupils concerned displaying greater awareness of their cultural identity in the host society. The scheme has helped them to become actively involved in collective tasks and taught them to resolve conflict through dialogue, using the appropriate language. It has also helped pupils develop tolerance and respect for others, their ideas, beliefs and opinions. It has helped pupils address certain social problems (intolerance, xenophobia, immigration). The teacher has a key role in the planning stage and in teaching pupils the conceptual content, related to procedures and behaviour/attitudes. It is important that the curriculum be open-ended, so that the teacher can adapt their approach to the actual conditions in the school. It is also important to involve the families, as far as possible, in order to facilitate and reinforce the learning process.

Creating a safe learning environment: celebrating similarities and differences (United Kingdom)

Context

A primary school in London with a multicultural, transient population, living in an area of deprivation. It can be used in humanities lessons (history, geography, religious education) or as part of a special week of activities like Refugee week, Black history week. It is best used at the beginning of a term when the teacher establishes a climate that celebrates pupils and their identities.

Objectives

The aim of the lesson is to create a safe learning environment where all pupils, their cultures, religions and identities, are valued and where pupils feel they have a common sense of belonging. This is achieved through sensitive and emotionally intelligent teacher-mediated learning, appropriate use of the voice, use of non-verbal cues, gestures and tone to enable all to feel included. The teacher's capacity to be objective and non-judgemental is critical to make this activity effective. The sensitive classroom environment sets the tone for pupil talk and their development as thinkers. Religion and identity go hand in hand, and a safe environment allows pupils to engage in a reciprocative dialogue in which their own and others' faith may be valued. The proverb "Our mind is like a parachute: it only works when it is open" is very important here. Skills of being a good listener are crucial to promote and demonstrate interest, celebration and unconditional empathy in being valued. This sets the basis of an understanding that religious education is about developing worldviews. RE allows the pupils the opportunity to see a wider world and investigate and experience it. Mutual boundaries of respect and confidentiality need to be set. It is important to avoid tokenism.

For pupils

- To become confident about their own identity and uniqueness.
- To recognise and value over time the diversity in their classroom.
- To develop knowledge and understanding of the global diaspora and links with other countries.

- To realise that faith and identity are not local phenomena but occur everywhere.

Teaching strategies

- Pupils sit in a circle to be visible to one another and promote a sense of class identity.
- Teaching is inclusive because the activities are accessible to pupils with special needs and disabilities.
- Use of modelling clay or plaster, photographs and displays means that language levels are not a barrier.
- Collaborative learning is used in group work, encouraging and praising one another, guiding and supporting one another, with full participation so that dominance and passivity are reduced.
- Parental, family and community participation is another strategy. This activity uses the pupil's family and community, and helps them feel part of the school. This helps pupils to value them and their learning. It also creates partnerships and reduces tensions.

Partnership

This activity was instigated by the class teacher in the school, in co-operation with the teacher responsible for Ethnic Minority Achievement (EMA).

Themes addressed

- Making all feel included and valued.
- Differences and similarities between people from different cultural and religious backgrounds.

Target group/size of group

A whole class of about 30 pupils, aged between 5 and 7.

Persons involved

The teacher, any support staff working with the teacher, the pupils, visitors such as parents and grandparents with their oral testimonies to faith and cultures.

Time needed for preparation and implementation

One hour for preparation and about one to two hours for implementation. This includes the introduction to the activity, varying oral testimonies from visitors, pupil dialogue, then the actual activity work for display.

Description of activity

First, there is the setting of the verbal and non-verbal cues to create the safe climate and environment in preparation for the rest of the activity. Pupils then go on to talk about our commonality and differences – being part of one class, in one area, region, country, involves links with other countries in different parts of the world. Seeing language and religion in a global context, for example not all Hindus come from India, they live in the UK, Caribbean, etc. They come from different backgrounds and practise differently.

Pupils talk about their uniqueness; they use mirrors to observe features unique to them. They draw themselves.

Pupils talk about their grandparents – where they come from. They listen to the stories of parents or grandparents visiting the class – where they grew up, the songs they sang, the people they were influenced by, etc. They then link themselves to parts of the UK and different parts of the world.

They are then plotted onto a display/map of the world.

Pupils discuss how their families have come together in this place from different places, and realise what a diverse mixture produces the similarities of being together in one class. This is a cause of celebration.

Teaching/pedagogical materials and equipment used

Paper, drawing implements, mirrors, large map, tape to connect pictures to places on map.

Appraisal

One of the most fundamental lessons derived from this activity was recognising and valuing the strength of diversity of various faiths, and diversity within each faith. This contributed significantly to learning about and from religion. The challenge for many non-specialist teachers of RE is lack of subject knowledge. However, the pupils to some extent can help overcome this as they share beliefs and experiences common to them in relation to their faith. This minimises the "all Muslims, Hindus or Christians believe ..." but emphasises the individual; it marginalises stereotypes and labelling but personalises the pupils and their voices. The activity was very valuable in raising the self-esteem of pupils and their awareness of the value of others. It led to a notable increase in their awareness of the wider world. Their skills of empathising with each other increased. The pupils enjoyed the lesson, both in thinking about themselves in their drawings and in plotting the variety of places where families came from. They asked questions about the different places and different practices explained by the visitors. The ideas in this activity can be transferred to emphasise globalisation of religion and culture as well as variety of religion and culture locally. It will be applicable in different contexts or/and other national systems.

Advice

The activity could be improved by bigger displays (see pictures), or by being tailored to the preference of the teacher by using different media, for example photographs, plasticine, etc. The work aims to reduce or eliminate racist, cultural and religious prejudice, by empowering and valuing all pupils, not just the disadvantaged and vulnerable. The activity is not just multicultural but develops a collaborative approach where the community of pupils sets the scene for constructive discourse and valuing of diversity. An analogy with a flower may be helpful. The flower represents education. A flower's quality becomes apparent when it has fragrance. The fragrance of education is its "hidden" curriculum promoting respect and flourishing common to all humans. Education and intercultural valuing go together like a flower and its fragrance. Not only does the teacher have to achieve the highest standards of education for her pupils, but she has to educate them in relation to emotional intelligence, social codes, relationships, citizenship, tolerance and respect, whilst retaining identity and religion, in order to achieve this. The twin concepts of community and diversity, allowing for unity and difference, are vital for future citizens to live in harmony. The controversies which are inherent in this need to be turned into assets and opportunities.

Analysing simulated situations: what is respect? (United Kingdom)

Context

These lessons are part of a scheme to enable pupils in RE in England to think through issues of respect in plural societies. They are suited to citizenship lessons or RE lessons in lower secondary schools.

Learning objectives

Pupils should be able to:

*   learn from situations which demand respect across religious and cultural boundaries to explore attitudes, religious perspectives and ideas;
*   evaluate and deepen their own ideas about the concept of respect for all;
*   use the teachings of different religions to examine the concept of respect in depth.

Teaching strategies / group dynamics

Pupils work in pairs on nine situations where respect is needed, but not shown. They make judgements as they go.

Working methods

Group and individual work.

Themes addressed

*   Respect for and tolerance of others.
*   Empathy.

Target group/size of group

Class group of about 30 aged 14 years.

Persons involved

Teacher and pupils.

Time needed

Preparation: 20 minutes, implementation: two lessons of 40 minutes.

Description of activity

1. Work through the nine situations given below in a pair.

2. Discuss the alternatives to each situation – what could have happened if there was total disrespect? What could have happened if there was total respect?

3. Give a mark out of 10 to the person named in each box. 10 = gives plenty of respect. 1 = gives disrespect. Use a full range of marks.

4. Discuss your marks with other pairs: can a class agreement be reached?

5. Activities to follow up the learning:

- Put the nine characters in a rank order, from "most respectful" to "least respectful".

- There are various kinds of disrespect: racism and sexism are two. What kind of disrespect lies behind each of these nine situations?

- Arrange the class into nine small groups, and dramatise the situations given. Use a "freeze frame" strategy to stop the action at key moments, and ask those involved what their character would be thinking just then.

- Look at the teachings of faith about respect for all in the bubbles. Who, in the situations you've looked at, needs to learn from the Buddhists, Christians, Hindus and Muslims? What might they learn?

- Write (in pairs?) two more situations which happen in school where respect is needed. Make them about the same length as these nine. Share the best ones with the class.

- Examine some religious teachings about respect and human dignity, to discern whether religions have good advice for us on this topic.

- Think carefully about your own attitudes: we all say we believe in respect, but we all fail to show it or do it sometimes. Discuss with a partner a time when you showed respect, and a time when you didn't.

- What would make for a more respectful school? What would teachers, pupils, and others have to do to make your school a more respectful place? Draw up a five-point plan and send it to the School Council if you like.

If you want to re-use these worksheets, get pupils to note their scores on separate paper.

Pedagogical material and equipment used

See the sheets below.

Appraisal

This approach to considering respect is rooted in pupils' own lives, draws attention to religious aspects of intercultural diversity and education, and is simply implemented in any classroom by a teacher willing to try active learning.

Tangible results: in action, we have found this work is a good way to open conversations about the meaning of respect in concrete and stimulating ways, including the religious dimensions of intercultural education. Pupils enjoyed the work.

We have published the activity to our subscribers, and from them have received feedback that it is practical, user-friendly and thought-provoking.

How can the activity be evaluated? Teachers can evaluate this work through discussion with students, or by setting written questions about the learning: what did you do? What were your thoughts? What did you learn?

Suggestions for transfer

Teachers for whom these situations are distant or dissimilar to those faced in their own national context might create scenarios of disrespect closer to the needs of their learners. They might write situations that correspond to the issues their pupils face, or those which use case studies from local or national news to stimulate values, clarification and thought about the impact of respectful attitudes.

Wisdom sayings from many traditions of faith and belief could be used to counterpoint the situations.

A. Jonathan and Iqbal have had three fights this year at school. Last time, both were suspended. Jonathan runs into Iqbal in the playground at Thursday break, and sends him flying. Iqbal stands up, and as the blood oozes from his knee he takes a deep breath; "Tell me you didn't mean that will you?" he says, in a challenging tone. There is a tense pause. "Sorry mate – didn't mean it," says Jonathan. They go their separate ways. Jonathan's respect score: [ ]	B. Sian is an Irish girl in an English class, the only one. Lots of her classmates tell Irish jokes, and usually she ignores the implications that she is a member of a stupid nationality. But on Thursday when Mr Jackman, a teacher, told a joke like this, she was offended, and refused to do any more of the Maths work until he apologised. Mr Jackman wouldn't apologise, and said Sian was "being disruptive". He sent her to the head of year, and excluded her from Maths classes for the rest of the week. Mr Jackson's respect score: [ ]	C. In the playground, a gang of bullies often look at your trainers, and "tax" anyone who isn't wearing the ones they approve of. This Tuesday, Gang Big Cheese Derek picks on Hannah: "Your trainers look like damaged dog paws, you uncool person. We require you to pay 50p tax. Cough up." Hannah is having none of it, and boldly replies: "Your face looks like a damaged dog's backside, bully. Leave me alone." There is a short silence, but then Derek decides not to push it. He laughs and leaves. Derek's respect score: [ ]
D. Ms Hussain, the supply teacher, is getting a bit of trouble from class F. After a whole week in which they have been rude and unhelpful, on Friday morning one of them shouts out to her: "Miss, you're a Muslim, you ain't supposed to be working today – it's Friday, you don't work on Fridays do you?" Ms Hussain looks red in the face, but is silent. David, who has joined in with the bad behaviour all week, suddenly speaks up for her: "Shut up, it's her religion, she can't help it. You've got to respect her religion." David's respect score: [ ]	E. It is the class RE trip to the Hindu Mandir: on entry everyone is asked to take off their shoes. Sharon and Karen leave their gorgeous costly footwear in the Temple shoe racks, but moan in whispers all morning about the requirement. "Why should we take our shoes off? We don't worship their gods and goddesses, so why do we have to leave our shoes? They're nice shoes: someone might nick them!" But they say nothing out loud, and at the end they thank their Hindu hosts for having them. Their shoes are still where they left them. Sharon and Karen's respect score: [ ]	F. It is the school end of term Talent Show. Some of the acts are excellent, but several are dodgy. On the back row, year 9 boys are seated, and laugh about the undetectability of shouting "Rubbish" "You talentless nobody" and similar at some of the year 7 dance acts. Darryl decides not to join in – "At least they've got the guts to get up on the stage," he tells his mates, "Unlike you, hiding on the back row in the dark." His mates tell him he's a wimp, but he doesn't care, and keeps quiet, applauding the good acts, but not dissing the less good ones. Darryl's respect score: [ ]

G. Rose is a traveller girl, and joins her year 8 class three weeks into term. She is rather alone, and doesn't have many good friends at the school. After a couple of weeks of term, Anna (a bit of a leader in the class, never short of an opinion) picks on Rose with a bit of advice: "You're never going to make friends in this school unless you start acting like a friendly person, and not keeping your own precious Gypsy culture to yourself." Rose feels very anxious – but she replies "You won't make friends with me if you start by dishing out advice Anna." The girls eye each other up for a moment, and then Anna says "OK, well we're going to the cinema on Saturday. D'you want to come?"

Anna's respect score: [ ]

H. At the school disco, Kelly spent a long time showing off to some lads from year 11, but when she went outside with Jamie, one of them, it wasn't what she expected, and she told her mates the next day: "He has no respect for a girl. Don't let him get near you. He's about as attractive as a baboon's armpit." Jamie spends the day telling his friends and any other lads who will listen that Kelly is a baby: "She is about as mature as an egg," he says.

Kelly's respect score: [ ]
Jamie's respect score: [ ]

I. In a year 10 Food technology class, there are 24 girls and two boys. In the Technical graphics class there are 24 boys and two girls. At the School Council, Jo and Mark ask the teachers if the school's option groups are sexist, and offer to do a student survey about sexism in the subjects. The head teacher and a governor agree to this, and Jo and Mark organise the survey as part of their citizenship studies. They report that the school options system is biased and sexist, and not enough is done to make it possible for boys and girls to choose subjects against stereotypes.

Jo and Mark's respect score: [ ]

Buddhists say:

"Compassion for all beings is close to the heart of the Buddha's teaching. We want to be aware of anything which hurts others, and practise meditation to live harmlessly. We aim to find a way of life where right speech and right action do show respect for all, as the Buddha taught us."

Christians say:

"Our scripture says that in Christ there is no male or female, Jew or Greek, slave or free person – we are to live as one family. Christians should be the last to be prejudiced, because we believe God loves everyone with boundless love, and we seek to try to do the same."

Hindus say:

"There is a divine spark in all life, so we should respect the fire of the gods that burns in all brothers and sisters everywhere. Many Hindu heroes and stories remind us that a god may come to you in the form of beggar or outcast – so treat all people fairly to honour the spark of god within."

Muslims say:

"Allah is the creator of all, so no human has reason to despise another. Allah is the judge of all, so all humans should take responsibility for their attitudes to others. Allah is the most merciful, so even if someone wrongs you, you can learn a lesson, and be merciful yourself. Islam gives a good foundation to respect between all the world's people."

Using a national arts competition: creative work on religious dimensions of intercultural education (United Kingdom)

Context

The "Spirited Arts" competition, run successfully and nationally in England (with some entries from other parts of the UK) proposed four themes for art work in classroom contexts 5-16 (both religious education and art were used as contexts, often working together). Teachers interpreted these flexible themes in many ways. The online "Art in Heaven" Gallery enables the young people's artistic reflections to be shared and disseminated in wide and inspiring circles.

Learning objectives

- To connect themes in religion and intercultural education and promote interreligious education.
- To identify turning points in a religious story.
- To encourage creativity in this work by designing logos.
- To stimulate effective thinking and understanding about the intercultural and interreligious aspects of citizenship.
- With regard to the religions studied, pupils learn to explore and respond to the teachings about respect for all.
- To develop skills of self-expression (visual and literary) and consider the impact of attitudes from religions to other people on life and practice, including their own.

Partners

The Professional Council for Religious Education (PCfRE) is the main RE teachers' association in the UK. It used a funding source – the Westhill Trust – to work with hundreds of teachers in schools.

Teaching strategies / group dynamics

PCFRE proposed the competition, devised the themes, announced and gathered support for the activity through its networks. It established and maintains the website of associated pupils' work as a "web gallery". It disseminated the theme of "designing a logo for interreligious understanding" to many schools and colleges across the 5-17 age range, using the text below.

Themes addressed

Peace.

Target group/size of group

Ages 7-14, groups of up to 30 at a time.

Persons involved

Art teachers, RE teachers, Citizenship teachers.

Time needed for preparation

30 minutes.

Time needed for implementation

1-2 hours + homework.

Description of the activity

a. Talk about the theme of peace.

Peace is central to religious dimensions of intercultural education in many ways – pupils could learn about the inner peace which Christians seek through prayer, or the stillness and tranquillity Buddhists find through meditation. But inner peace and peace in the world are contrasts – and the ethics of peace and conflict give other angles on the theme.

1. Talking to pupils about the meanings of peace is a good beginning for this topic. Questions such as "What does it mean to have peace through the storm?" "Where is peace to be found?" "Does God bring peace?" and "How can anyone be peaceful when the world is so troubled?" are the stuff of good intercultural education, and make good "launchers" for this work.

2. Pupils will find it helpful to have a clear brief for this theme, which is of course very wide. Ask them to make a symbol for peace to use on a United Nations greetings card, or devise a logo for a divided city (Jerusalem? Belfast?) that is aiming for communal harmony, or a symbol for the peace of the heart. Ask them how the European intercultural project should devise a logo to include religious and non-religious visions of peace.

b. Design a logo for intercultural education about religion

1. This activity works well if you want pupils to think through what respect between religions means. We have tried it out in making new covers for RE Agreed Syllabuses in several parts of the country (UK). Talk to pupils about the ways in which religions co-operate and connect, alert to what is significant in each faith, but also drawing attention to how faiths share some values and ideas.

2. Ask them to design a logo or image that respects six different religions, and which shows what can be fun in religious dimensions of intercultural education. Look together at some symbols for different religions. Consider what balances and distinctive colours are good for different religions. Simple colour, considering alternatives carefully and looking at the ideas of others will stimulate better work. Give them the challenge to show their vision of all the religions, not just copy out a symbol nicely!

3. Make sure that they write a paragraph explaining what is good about the logo they have designed, and how it shows the spirituality of the religions and of themselves.

Pedagogical material and equipment used

*   The best art materials available to the group.
*   Opportunities to examine and respond to symbols and information from several religions.

Appraisal

The organisers consider it to be one of the most successful ways of encouraging reflective and sensitive learning with regard to religious aspects of intercultural education. Teachers engaged in the competition reported very high levels of interest, motivation and enthusiasm for the project from many pupils. The quality of work (see the website[19]) is representative of the best, but a very wide impact from the several hundred schools taking part is evident.

This highly successful project has energised the learning and spiritual thinking of many hundreds – thousands – of pupils in UK RE and Art settings, making them think about the ways we express co-operation and respect between religions.

19. www.pcfre.org.uk/spiritedarts.

The creative activity generates a context for exploring concepts such as mutual understanding, difference and similarity, cohesion and conflict, with some sensitivity. Teachers can use pupil groups, structured discussion and evaluation questions to focus this. Challenging quotations from sources within different religions, including sacred writings, can be presented as the focus for discussion.

Pupils will easily gather ideas, information and examples of, for example, Christian and Muslim understanding of tolerance and respect from their RE lessons, if they have them. If no RE lessons are provided, teachers may need to give pupils specific information.

Suggestions for transfer

Many other themes can be used. Pupils can examine the work of others from many traditions as an inspiration to their own.

Using building crafts: our house – our village – our world (Austria)

Context

The project was done to become a member of Pilgrim-Schule, which is a network of schools working on projects in the areas of economy, ecology, society and spirituality for a lasting change of the future. The school is situated in the 10th district in Vienna with pupils from different cultures and religions. The project was started to improve appreciation of and to learn about the different cultures in the daily integrative work.

Objectives

- Pupils to make their own decisions.

- Being environmentally sensitive.

- Becoming self-confident and self-determined regarding the requests of the group.

- Participation in the activities of the project.

- Making the principal attitudes of society visible by using the following principles in the daily routines:

    i. a tolerant and appreciative attitude to all others;

    ii. thinking and acting in a self-confident way;

    iii. being always willing to search for compromise;

    iv. constructive co-operation within the group, even if their own targets cannot be reached;

    v. never to allow others to control their own life;

    vi. never to think that violence can solve any problem;

    vii. never to think that somebody else is necessarily best.

- The perception that nothing can be solved by competing, but nearly everything can be achieved with good team work, so it should be a real help in the further life of the pupils and protect them.

Teaching strategies

Two classes (little more than 50 pupils) were divided into 10 family groups without giving concrete instructions on how to create their social life. The only requirement was to finish their own small house (1.5 m x 2 m x 2 m: only the wooden frame), within the next two years. Changing members of the groups was not allowed even when problems occurred. The houses were grouped in three and were oriented to the "Hauptplatz" (main area) where all entrances were located. The pupils had to decide how to add the walls, the floor, the windows and the doors. They could ask questions, but didn't get other support. The teachers had to ensure that the decisions within the groups were made in a democratic way and the rules were kept.

Appraisal

The pupils were very proud of "their" houses when they were finished, so they wanted to use them outside the official "project hours" as well. Therefore they got the opportunity to move on, as soon as they had finished their exercises. Later group examinations and activities for other projects were done by "living" in the houses. As they were most comfortable, the daily main break, where they take their lunch, was spent staying in their houses and talking about them.

Ongoing activities

After the houses were finished, the next activity was to organise an exhibition about the world's religions. Here parents, coming from different regions in the world, worked together with pupils and teachers. At the opening, dishes from all areas of the world were presented. This was done in special ceremonies. Of course the pupils also presented their houses and a lot of interesting stories were told.

PART V
REFERENCES

Bibliography

Afdal, G., Haakedal, E., and Leganger-Krogstad, H. (eds.), *Tro, livstolkning og tradisjon: innføring i kontekstuell religionsdidaktikk* (Faith, life philosophy and tradition: an introduction to a contextual approach to religious education), Tano Aschehoug, Oslo, 1997.

"Intercultural learning T-kit", Council of Europe and European Commission, Council of Europe Publishing, 2000, ISBN 92-871-534-7.

"The religious dimension of intercultural education: Conference proceedings, Oslo, Norway 6-8 June 2004", Division for the European Dimension in Education, Council of Europe Publishing, 2004, ISBN 92-871-5622-0.

Ballard, R. (ed.), *Desh Pardesh: the South Asian presence in Britain*, Hurst and Co., London, 1994.

Barratt, M., *An Egg for Babcha*, "Bridges to Religions" series, *The Warwick RE Project,* Heinemann, Oxford, 1994a.

__ *Lucy's Sunday*, Bridges to Religions series, *The Warwick RE Project*, Heinemann, Oxford, 1994b.

__ *Something to share*, Bridges to Religions series, *The Warwick RE Project*, Heinemann, Oxford, 1994c.

__ *The Buddha's birthday*, Bridges to Religions series, *The Warwick RE Project*, Heinemann, Oxford, 1994d.

__ *The seventh day is Shabbat*, Bridges to Religions series, *The Warwick RE Project,* Heinemann, Oxford, 1994e.

Barth, F. (ed.), *Ethnic groups and boundaries*, Allen and Unwin, London, 1969.

Barth, F., "Ethnic groups and boundaries", in *Process and forms in social life: Selected essays,* Routledge and Kegan Paul, London, 1981.

Baumann, G., *Contesting culture: discourses of identity in multi-ethnic London*, Cambridge University Press, Cambridge, 1996.

Beckford, J. and Gilliat, S., *Religion in prisons: equal rites in a multi-faith society*, Cambridge University Press, London, 1998.

Benedict, R., *Patterns of culture*, Routledge and Kegan Paul, London, 1935. Berkeley, 1986, pp. 194-233.

Bevans, S.B., *Models of contextual theology*, Orbis Books, Maryknoll, NY, 1992.

Bickford, S., *The dissonance of democracy*, Cornell University Press, Ithaca, 1996.

Bohman, J., *Public deliberation*, MIT Press, Cambridge, 1996.

Brunstad, P.O., *Ungdom og livstolkning: en studie av unge menneskers tro og fremtidsforventninger* (Youth and life-interpretation: a study of young people's faith and their expectations for the future), Tapir, Trondheim, 1998.

Carens, J., "Immigration et démocratie libérale", *Pluralisme, citoyenneté et éducation* (sous la direction de Gagnon, McAndrew et Pagé), Harmattan, Montreal, 1997, pp. 95-120.

Clifford, J., "Introduction: partial truths", in J. Clifford and G. Marcus, eds., *Writing culture: the poetics and politics of ethnography*, University of California Press, Berkeley, 1986, pp. 1-26.

Clifford, J., *The predicament of culture*, Harvard University Press, Cambridge, MA, 1988.

Dashefsky, A., "And the search goes on: religio-ethnic identity and identification", *Sociological Analysis*, Vol. 33, No. 4, 1972, pp. 239-45.

EDC pack, Council of Europe 2005: http://www.coe.int/T/E/Cultural_Co-operation/education/E.D.C/documents_and_publications/EDC_Pack/default.asp#TopOfPage

Fischer, M.M.J., "Ethnicity and the post-modern arts of memory", in J. Clifford and G. Marcus (eds.), *Writing culture: the poetics and politics of ethnography*, University of California Press.

Freire, P., *Pedagogy of the oppressed*, Penguin, London, 1996.

Heimbrock, H.-G., *Religionsunterricht im Kontext Europa. Einführung in die Kontextuelle Religionsdidaktik in Deutschland*, Kohlhammer, Stuttgart, 2004.

Gadamer, H.-G., *Truth and method*, Seabury Press, New York, 1975.

Geertz, C., *Local knowledge*, Basic Books, New York, 1983.

Geertz, C., *The interpretation of cultures*, Basic Books, New York, 1973.

Giddens, A., *Sociology*, 2nd edn, Polity Press, Cambridge, 1993.

Grimmitt, M., Grove, J., Hull, J. and Spencer, L., *A gift to a child*, University of Birmingham, 1996.

Gutmann, A. and Thompson, D., *Democracy and disagreement*, Harvard University Press, Cambridge, 1996.

Gutmann, A., *"Civic education and social diversity"*, Ethics, 105, pp. 555-579.

Ipgrave, J., *Building E-Bridges*, Birmingham Christian Education Movement, 2003.

Ipgrave, J., *Pupil-to-pupil dialogue in the classroom as a tool for religious education,* Warwick Religions and Education Research Unit Working Papers, 2, University of Warwick, Coventry, 2001.

Jackson R., *Din Egitimi: Yorumlayıcı Bir Yaklaşım. Değerler Eğitimi Merkezi Yayınları*, 2005a (Turkish translation of *Religious education: an interpretive approach*).

Jackson, R. (ed.), *International perspectives on citizenship, education and religious diversity*. Routledge Falmer, London, 2003.

Jackson, R. and Nesbitt, E.M., *Hindu children in Britain,* Trentham, Stoke on Trent, 1993.

Jackson, R., "Intercultural education and recent European pedagogies of religious Education", *Intercultural Education* 15 (1), 2004b, pp. 3-14.

Jackson, R., "Intercultural education and religious diversity: interpretive and dialogical approaches from England", in Council of Europe (ed.), *The religious dimension of intercultural education*, Council of Europe Publishing, Strasbourg, 2004d, pp. 39-50.

Jackson, R., "L'approche interprétative en enseignement religieux: une pédagogie de la compréhension interculturelle", in Fernand Ouellet (ed.) *Quelle formation pour l'éducation à la religion?* Les Presses de l'Université Laval, Quebec, 2005c, pp. 119-143.

Jackson, R., "L'éducation interculturelle et la diversité religieuse: les approches interprétatives et dialogiques en Angleterre" in Fernand Ouellet (ed.) *Quelle formation pour l'éducation à la religion?* Les Presses de l'Université Laval, Quebec, 2005b, pp. 105-118.

Jackson, R., "Studying religious diversity in public education: an interpretive approach to religious and intercultural understanding", *Religion and Education* (USA), 2004c, pp. 1-20.

Jackson, R., "The construction of 'Hinduism' and its impact on religious education in England and Wales", *Panorama: International Journal of Comparative Religious Education and Values*, Vol. 8, No. 2, 1996, pp. 86-104.

Jackson, R., *Religious education: an interpretive approach*, Hodder & Stoughton, London, 1997.

Jackson, R., *Rethinking religious education and plurality: issues in diversity and pedagogy*, Routledge Falmer, London, 2004a, Chapter 6.

Jacobson, J., "Religion and ethnicity: dual and alternative sources of identity among young British Pakistanis", *Ethnic and Racial Studies*, Vol. 20, No. 2, 1997, pp. 238-256.

Jensen, T., "The religiousness of Muslim pupils in Danish upper-secondary schools", in Shadid, W.A.R. and Van Koningsveld, P.S. (eds.), *Intercultural relations and religious authorities: Muslims in the European Union*, Peeters, Leuven, 2002, pp. 123-137.

Jones, R. and Welengama, G., *Ethnic minorities in English law*, Trentham, Stoke on Trent, 2000.

Keast, A., and Keast, J., *Framework RE, Book I,* Hodder Headline, London, 2005.

Kristiansen, R.E., *Religion i kontekst: bidrag til en nordnorsk teologi* (Religion in context: a contribution to a northern Norwegian theology), Norges forskningsråd, Oslo, 1996.

Valk, P., *Eesti kooli religiooniõpetuse kontseptsioon* (Contextual approach in Estland), *Theologiae Universitatis Tartuensis*, Universitatis Tartuensis, Tartu, 2002.

Leganger-Krogstad, H., "Religious Education in a global perspective: a contextual approach", in H.-G. Heimbrock, C.T. Scheilke and P. Schreiner (eds.), *Towards religious competence: diversity as a challenge for education in Europe*, LIT Verlag, Münster, Hamburg, Berlin, London, 2001, pp. 53-73.

Leganger-Krogstad, H., Mikkelsmess: En kirke, fem skoler og et nærmiljø (St Michael's Mass: one Church, five schools and a local community), *Prismet*, 54(2), 2003, pp. 69-73.

Leganger-Krogstad, H., *Læstadianske oppdragelsesidealer og skolekonflikten i Alta: foreldrenes ønsker for opplæring og oppdragelse* (The Laestadians' ideals for upbringing and the school conflict in Alta: the parents' view on education and nurture), Høgskolen i Finnmark Avdeling for barnehage-og skolefag, Alta, 1995.

Leganger-Krogstad, H., "Ethnic minority in conflict with Norwegian educational ideals", *PANORAMA International Journal of Comparative Religions Education and Values* 10 (1), 1998, pp. 131-145.

Leganger-Krogstad, H., "Developing a contextual theory and practice of religious education", *PANORAMA International Journal of Comparative Religions Education and Values* 12(1), 2000, pp. 94-104.

Locke, J., *Lettre sur la tolérance*, Paris, Quadrige/PUF, 1999.

Mercier, Carrie, *Muslims*, "Interpreting Religions" series, *The Warwick RE Project,* Heinemann, Oxford, 1996.

Modood, T., "'Difference', cultural racism and anti-racism", in P. Werbner and T.

Modood (eds.), *Debating cultural hybridity*, Zed Books, London, 1997, pp. 154-172.

Nesbitt, E., *Intercultural education: ethnographic and religious approaches*, Sussex Academic Press, Brighton, 2004.

O'Grady, K. (2003), "Motivation in religious education: a collaborative investigation with year eight students", *British Journal of Religious Education* 25 (3), pp. 214-225.

Østberg, S., *The nurture of Pakistani Muslim children in Oslo,* Monograph Series, University of Leeds, Leeds, Community Religions Project, 2003.

Rawls, J., *Libéralisme politique*, Paris, PUF (translated from *Political liberalism*, Columbia University Press, New York, 1993), 1995.

Religious Education: The Non-Statutory Framework, published by Qualifications and Curriculum Authority, London, 2004, Reference No. QCA/04/1336.

Rey, M., "Human rights and intercultural education" in H. Starkey (ed.), *The Challenge of Human Rights Education*, Cassell and Council of Europe, London, 1991, pp. 135-151.

Ricoeur, P., *Time and Narrative*, Vol. 3. University of Chicago Press, Chicago/London, 1988.

Robson, G., *Christians*, "Interpreting Religions" series, *The Warwick RE Project*, Heinemann, Oxford, 1995.

Said, E., *Orientalism*, Routledge and Kegan Paul, London, 1978.

Senge, P. et al., *Schools that learn*, A fifth discipline fieldbook for educators, parents and everyone who cares about education, Doubleday, New York, 2000.

Skeie, G., "Plurality and pluralism: a challenge for religious education", *British Journal of Religious Education*, Vol. 25, No. 1, 1995, pp. 47-59.

Smith, W.C., *The meaning and end of religion*, SPCK, London, 1978.

Vygotskij, L.S., Rieber, R.W. et al., *The collected works of L.S. Vygotsky*, Plenum Press, New York, 1987.

Wayne, E., Everington, J., Kadodwala, D. and Nesbitt, E., *Hindus*, "Interpreting Religions" series, *The Warwick RE Project,* Heinemann, Oxford, 1996.

Weber, M., *Économie et société*, Vols. I and II, Plon, Paris, 1971.

Weber, M., *Le savant et le politique*, La Découverte/Poche, Paris, 2003.

Weithman, P.J., *Religion and the Obligations of Citizenship*, Cambridge University Press, Cambridge, 2002.

Textbooks and teaching resources

The following is a list of various information and practical teaching material resources for teachers, examples of learning activities, etc.

Abrami, P.C. et al., *L'apprentissage coopératif – Théories, méthodes, activités.* Centre d'études sur l'apprentissage en classe, Université Concordia, Les Éditions de la Chenelière inc., Montreal, 1996.

The first part of this collection of papers sets out the relevant concepts – theoretical foundations and teaching approaches – for a better understanding of co-operative learning. The two other sections – the most current methods and practical applications – provide insight into practical concerns, dealing both with problems and solutions.

Bradford Metropolitan District Council et al., *Regarding religion, Ideas for school classroom and community, partnership in education for citizenship and shared values,* Bradford Education, Bradford, 1998.

Bundeszentrale für politische Bildung, Dialog der Religionen und Weltanschauungen. Herausforderung an die Demokratie, Themen und Materialien Arbeitshilfen für die politische Bildung, Bundeszentrale für politische Bildung, Berlin, 2003.

Bundeszentrale für politische Bildung, Erwachsenwerden vor dem Hintergrund unterschiedlicher Religionen und Weltanschauungen, Themen und Materialien Arbeitshilfen für die politische Bildung, Bundeszentrale für politische Bildung, Berlin, 2004.

These two publications are the result of a dialogue between people from different religions organised by the Workshop Religions and World Views in the Workshop of Cultures in Berlin. It includes basic texts and modules that can be used in schools and other pedagogical institutions.

Cohen, E.G., *"Equity in heterogeneous classrooms: a challenge for teachers and sociologists",* Working for equity in heterogeneous classrooms – Sociological theory in practice. E.G. Cohen and R.A. Lotan (eds.), Sociology of Education Series, Teachers' College Press, Columbia University, New York and London, 1997a, pp. 3-14.

This first chapter of the monograph is an introduction to the concepts of complex instruction and equitable classrooms. It places research in the broader context of classroom stratification and sociology.

Cohen, E.G., *"The social construction of equity in the classroom"*, Les défis du pluralisme en éducation: essais sur la formation interculturelle. Fernand Ouellet, with a contribution by E. Cohen. Presses de l'Université Laval, Sainte-Foy, 2002.

This chapter deals in greater depth with the concept of the "equitable classroom" by showing how to bring it about through the application of certain principles. The author examines the problem of diversity in the classroom, dealing with problems of "status", supervision of teachers in the classroom and further training for teachers. It also looks at theory and research.

Cohen, E.G., *"Understanding status problems: sources and consequences"*, Working for equity in heterogeneous classrooms – Sociological theory in practice. E.G. Cohen and R.A. Lotan (eds.), Sociology of Education Series, Teachers' College Press, Columbia University, New York and London, 1997b, pp. 61-76.

This chapter focuses on dealing with status problems in the classroom, offering theoretical explanations on the nature of this type of problem. The author offers explanations on the process of generalisation and on interaction and statuses in the context of complex instruction.

Cohen, E.G., *Designing group work: strategies for the heterogeneous classroom*, Teachers' College Press, New York, 1986.

This reference book is designed to encourage pupil participation in the classroom, especially in heterogeneous groups. It illustrates how pupils can learn, share and contribute more actively when the class is geared to group work. The reference book considers the problems inherent in this approach and offers practical solutions.

Gaudet, D. et al., *La coopération en classe – Guide pratique appliqué à l'enseignement quotidien*. Chenelière/McGraw-Hill, Montreal and Toronto, 1998.

The main part of this compendium is devoted to activities and lesson plans, with worksheets and a list of material required. The subjects covered tie in with the curriculum laid down by the Quebec Ministry of Education. The authors also shed light on the characteristics of co-operation in the classroom.

Giroux, F., *"La coopération en contexte pluraliste",* La coopération dans la classe. M.-F. Daniel and M. Shleifer (eds.), Les Éditions Logiques, Canada, 1995, pp. 249-284.

The author of this chapter first of all discusses the many varied co-operation approaches and then makes a theoretical analysis of co-operative learning in a multi-ethnic context. The second part discusses equal opportunities in education, conflict, acquisition of equal status and anti-racism.

Green, N. and Green, K., *Kooperatives Lernen im Klassenraum und im Kollegium.* Ein Trainingsbuch, Velber, Kallmeyer bei Friedrich, 2005.

This book offers exercises for introducing, organising and evaluating group learning processes to facilitate heterogeneous groups to work together. The authors write on the background of long-standing experience in school education in Durham, Ontario, Canada.

Greminger Kost, E., Halfhide, E. and Mächler, S. (eds.), *Religionen und ihre Feste. Ein Leitfaden durch das interkulturelle Schuljahr*, Verlag Pestalozzianum, Zurich, 1998.

A guide for teachers with a calendar of the religious festivals to be used throughout the school year. It includes basic information about the world religions and about the festivals.

Howden, J. and Kopiec, M., *Ajouter aux compétences: enseigner, coopérer et apprendre au secondaire et au collégial,* Les éditions de la Chenelière/McGraw-Hill, Montreal and Toronto, 2000.

Howden, J. and Kopiec, M., *Cultiver la collaboration – Un outil pour les leaders pédagogiques*, Chenelière/McGraw-Hill, Montreal and Toronto, 2002.

This work focuses on setting up a co-operative framework in schools. It gives ideas on how to guide teaching staff. Topics covered include values, the role of lead teacher, teaching approaches, the various forms of collaboration in schools, career advancement, including the assessment of leaders, and peer support.

Howden, J. and Laurendeau, F., *La coopération: un jeu d'enfant – De l'apprentissage à l'évaluation*, Les éditions de la Chenelière/McGraw-Hill, Montreal and Toronto, 2005.

Howden, J. and Martin, H., *La coopération au fil des jours – Des outils pour apprendre à coopérer*, Les éditions de la Chenelière, Montreal, 1997.

Johnson, D.W., Johnson, R.T. and Johnson Holubec, E., *Cooperation in the Classroom* (7th edn), Interaction Book Company, Edina, MN, 1998.

The authors give an overview of the component parts of co-operative learning: definition, aims, learning processes, role of the teacher, and a short survey of research. It also provides some clarifications on positive interdependence; the skills required for co-operation, the organisation of groups, assessments, class management and suggested action. This book is a sound introduction to co-operative learning.

Kagan, S., *Cooperative learning: resources for teachers*, Resources for Teachers, San Juan Capistrano, CA, 1992.

Lehrmittelverlag des Kantons Zürich, Heilige Gesetze – *Lebensentwürfe. Interreligiöser Kalender, pädagogischer Leitfaden und Kartenset, Lehrmittelverlag,* Zurich, 2002/2003ff.

This material is published every year. It consists of a monthly calendar that informs about the festivals of the month with a short explanation. For each month a piece of information is added about one of the world religions. A pedagogical guide and a set of pictures are also available.

Sabourin, M. et al., *Coopérer pour réussir, Préscolaire et 1er cycle – Scénarios d'activités coopératives pour développer des compétences*, Les Éditions de la Chenelière/McGraw-Hill, Montreal and Toronto, 2002.

Shap Working Party (each year): *Calendar of religious festivals*

The Shap Calendar of Religious Festivals is an invaluable resource for the teaching profession, students, businesses, chaplaincies, those in health care and public services, to name but a few. It provides a colourful A2 wall planner, A5 laminated year planner with an accompanying A5 booklet, a brief description of each religious festival, an overview of 17 months from August of one year to December of the next, details on 12 different faiths from Baha'i to Zoroastrian (Parsee) and including Buddhism, Christianity, Islam, Hinduism, Judaism and Sikhism, a version from the European working party members with parallel text in French, English and German.

Contact: The Shap Working Party, PO Box 38580, London, SW1P 3XF, United Kingdom.

Shap Working Party, *Festivals in world religions*, edited by Peter Woodward with Riadh El-Droubie and Cherry Gould, Religious and Moral Education Press, Norwich, 1998.

A comprehensive reference book for primary and secondary schools. It provides accurate and detailed information on religious festivals celebrated around the world. Chapters describe Baha'i, Buddhist, Chinese, Christian, Hindu, Jain, Japanese, Jewish, Muslim, Sikh, and Zoroastrian/Parsi festivals.

Sharan, S., *"Co-operative learning and helping behaviour in the multi-ethnic classroom",* in H.C. Foot, M.J. Morgan and R.H. Shute (eds.), Children helping children, John Wiley and Sons, London, 1990, pp. 151-176.

Sieg, U., *Feste der Religionen.* Werkbuch für Schulen und Gemeinden, Patmos, Düsseldorf, 2003. Accurate information and narrative texts invite for encounter and dialogue among the different religions. The book has a special emphasis on relations between festivals of the different religions.

Slavin, R., *Cooperative learning: theory, research and practice,* Prentice Hall, Englewood Cliffs, NJ, 1990.

This book is a valuable contribution to the subject and presents the link between theory and practice in co-operative learning.

Slavin, R., *Using student team learning* (3rd edn) Johns Hopkins University, Centre for Research on Elementary and Middle Schools, Baltimore, MD, 1986.

This handbook is a result of an interfaith project (1995-98) which has involved teachers from five European cities. It contains examples of how teachers in five different cities have tried to bring children, parents, schools and the intercultural and interfaith communities they serve closer together by using material from the world's religions.

Totten, S. et al., *Cooperative learning – A guide to research,* Garland Publishing Inc., New York and London, 1991.

Bibliography broken down by subject – from information technology to career guidance, also covering social sciences, technology, and more general subjects such as the conditions conducive to co-operative work or research. The introduction gives an overview of literature on the subject.

Glossary

Some of the language used in this book might be new to some readers and/or teachers and so the authors decided to include this short glossary of terms to help them better understand the wider context. They should not be taken to be official definitions of the Council of Europe.

Accountability: responsibility for all contributions is important and essential for the success of the group activity.

Beliefs: propositions held as true by individuals and groups but not provable by evidence or reason beyond doubt; usually associated with a system of religious beliefs or philosophy.

Civic-mindedness: the first meaning of this concept relates to a citizen's attitude in public life. It does not refer to a regulatory ideal, but a means of coexistence which will bring about both respect and reciprocity, both of which presuppose a capacity for reflection and moderation in the public expression of one's convictions. It presupposes an ability to distance oneself from one's own convictions and beliefs.

Conviction: a strongly held opinion that may be religious or non-religious in character.

Co-operative learning: pedagogical approach based on the premise that no one can accomplish a task alone, and that it requires everyone to pull together in order to achieve a common goal.

De-culturation: removing of or a reduction in the effect of a culture or cultural influences.

Demotic discourse: the language of culture making, which often becomes used when people from various different backgrounds interact together in approaching topics of common concern.

Denomination: usually a sub-group of the Christian church, for example Roman Catholicism, but is also used to refer to any one religious group of another religion (for example Orthodox Judaism), or even used for a religion as a whole when distinct from another religion.

Dialogue: talking and listening to another. Used in this reference book to mean an educational instrument to avoid conflict – intercultural conflict in general and religious conflict in particular. The major role played by dialogue has given rise to an educational theory of dialogue, whose interdisciplinary nature reflects its many facets: religious, linguistic, social, ethical and so on. Focus is on communication and exchange. Can take place on different levels.

Distancing and simulations: kinds of learning that do not cause undue embarrassment, anxiety, or distress because they are "second-hand" and indirect forms of learning. They are sufficiently "removed" from the child and his or her own personal life, or from the actual community the child is from, that they allow study and learning to take place in a safe way, but at the same time they are close enough to the child and community to be realistic, meaningful and relevant to both the aims of study and the child's own capacity to understand and learn. Distancing and simulations involve role-play, simulation, imagination, research, resources, and rules.

Diversity: the presence of a variety of differences; these may be approaches, views, lifestyles, practices and attitudes that are different from each other, but exist in the same place, revealing difference. Diversity in the classroom relates to heterogeneous academic skills, linguistic skills and background, culture or religion.

Dominant discourse: to treat an abstract idea as though it were a concrete reality. Dominant discourse is often used by extremist groups, politicians, the media and by cultural communities themselves.

Empathetic communication: concept that can be incorporated into various teaching approaches in order to help young people understand others better. It is a dynamic mental and emotional stimulus that helps to get a better knowledge and understanding of others and oneself.

Ethnicity: the word ethnic – derived from *ethnos*, the Greek word for "nation" – is in common usage in English and has equivalents in some other European languages. A teacher thinking of moving to a new job might ask "What's the ethnic mix in the school?", "Which ethnic groups are represented?" In reporting the civil war in the former Yugoslavia, journalists used the chilling term "ethnic cleansing" for the first time. In these various cases, "ethnic" refers to *groups*, which, in principle, can interact with one another. Ethnicity can also refer to *categories*, for example in classifying members of a particular population by skin colour or by some other general category such as "Asian" or "Caucasian". As with "race" and "culture", "ethnicity" can be stereotyped in order to separate and isolate groups. It is therefore a term that needs to be used with caution.

Exclusive: an attitude that excludes others on the grounds of status, faith, class, or ethnicity.

Faith: an attitude of belief or trust, usually religious, and hence also used as an alternative for religion or religious tradition.

Globalisation: economic and cultural commonality and exchange across the world, which makes individual countries (or aspects of them) dependent on or similar to others.

Humanist: a view (or person holding the view) that meaning and purpose in life is the result of human rationality; there is no supernatural dimension to life.

Human rights: qualities and status accorded to all people simply by virtue of their being human, most often described in the European Convention on Human Rights.

Inclusion: an attitude (described as inclusive or inclusivist) that does not exclude others on the grounds of status, faith, class, or ethnicity.

Inter-religious: aspects of belief and practice that go across or lie between different religious traditions.

Intercultural: ideas, concepts, attitudes, practices and experiences that cross cultures; for example, the interactions between different cultures, the interdependence of different cultures.

Intercultural education: Such education needs to develop personal autonomy and a critical spirit, tolerance, openness to diversity and a feeling of belonging to the community as a whole. This type of education should ensure that it nurtures an understanding of the phenomena of both belief and non-belief and the ability to reflect on the different worldviews to be found in pluralist societies. It concerns the fundamental educational interests of children. These interests cover not only matters relating to general cognitive aptitudes but also a child's right to be prepared appropriately for life as a citizen playing a full part in democracy. It should also nurture a sense of trust uniting citizens beyond their moral and religious differences and disagreements. "Intercultural education" rather than "multicultural education" is used to emphasise a more critical view of culture than that used in early multicultural education.

Interpretive approach: pedagogical approach that takes account of the diversity that exists within religions and allows for the interaction of religion and culture, for change over time and for different views as to what a religion is.

Laïcité **(Laicity)**: a political concept deriving from France whereby the state is independent of any religious group, principle or practice in any way.

Modern: a characterisation of history and human living deriving from the Enlightenment, based on the role of reason in the study of history and ideas – hence modernity.

Monocultural: a society that largely consists of people sharing the same cultural or religious traditions.

Moral: a matter of right and wrong, often liked to ethics, the study of what is right and wrong.

Multicultural: the existence of a plurality of cultures side by side in the same state or society, but sometimes used in a loaded way either to imply an undesirable mix of different cultures that have no commonality or to imply a desirable blending of cultures to form a rich diversity.

Multi-faith: the existence of a plurality of religious or faith traditions in the same state or society.

Myth: commonly understood to mean not factually true but more properly a technical term for a story whose truth is of a religious or spiritual kind, deriving from the Greek *muthos* – the words that accompanied the drama in ancient ceremonies and rituals.

Nation-state: a "state" is usually regarded as a governed society, supported by a civil service, ruling over a specific area, and whose authority is supported by law and the ability to use force. Thus a "nation-state" is a variety of modern state, in which "the mass of the population are citizens who know themselves to be part of that nation" (Giddens 1993, p. 743). Perhaps this definition should be broadened, for a state can include groups who regard themselves as nations (comprised of one or more ethnic groups) and might aspire to their own statehood, as with Scottish, Welsh or Basque nationalism.

Pedagogy: the art or science of teaching, and the principles or methods behind the practice of teaching and learning.

Phenomenological approach: pedagogical approach that promotes knowledge, understanding and empathy, avoids imposing one's own views and attitudes upon another's, and tries to understand without judging.

Pluralism: normative idea based on interpretation and judgement, different from plurality, which is a descriptive concept.

Plurality: traditional plurality corresponds to the observable cultural diversity present in many western societies, usually resulting from the migration of peoples or, in certain cases, the presence of indigenous peoples. Modern or postmodern plurality relates to the varied intellectual climate of late modernity or postmodernity. This form of plurality reflects the fragmentation of societies, with various groups' competing, sometimes contradictory thought processes, and with individuals often choosing values and ideas from a variety of sources.

Positive interdependence: structure to ensure that pupils work together, where pupils are concerned not only about their own education but also that of their classmates.

Postmodern: a characterisation of thought and understanding deriving from developments in linguistics, philosophy and culture in the mid 20th century, which dispenses with grand ideas and philosophies (meta-narratives), objective understanding of truth and the dominance of reason.

Race: scientifically discredited term used in the past to describe what were believed to be biologically distinct groups of human beings.

Racism: refers to discrimination against others on the basis of their supposed membership of a "racial" group. Thus the underlying explanation of "racial" differences may be cultural or religious, for example, and not "biological". Some writers use the term "cultural racism" to emphasise this association of appearance with a stereotyped view of a culture or religion. Institutional racism has been defined as the collective failure of an organisation to provide an appropriate and professional service to people because of their colour, culture or ethnic origin which can be seen or detected in processes, attitudes and behaviour which amount to discrimination through unwitting prejudice, ignorance, thoughtlessness and racist stereotyping which disadvantages minority ethnic people.

Reciprocity: ability to think in terms of reciprocity is a social skill comprising a readiness to acknowledge or grant others the same things one would like to see recognised or granted for oneself and not to offend others on matters on which one would not wish to be offended oneself.

Reflexivity: critical feedback on conduct and its individual and group effects. Reflection should be introduced as a process in order to help young people adopt a position in a thoughtful, autonomous and responsible way in the light of their own values and the diversity of values.

Religion: generally an approach to life and the world based on a concept of the ultimate, transcendent, God or gods; specifically a system of beliefs, expression and practice, such as teachings, worship and lifestyle often associated with a revelation.

Religious education: a phrase referring to the provision of an education in religion, but interpreted and provided differently in different states of Europe. The main differences concern the nature and intention of such education; for example, whether it is "confessional" – a nurturing of a child into a religion and forming the child's religious affiliation, or whether it is "non-confessional" – an open and critical study, leaving the question of any religious affiliation to the child and/or family. Such differences are often related to the type of school (religious or common school) but also relate to the different arrangements that exist between the state and religious communities.

Respect: an attitude of a civil and courteous nature that values the Other.

Safe space: precondition of needed dialogue to explore differences in a context of security, freedom, and serenity in order to allow sharing, telling, listening or reconciling.

Sect: a subdivision of a religious or faith tradition, sometimes defined as a group where the emphasis is on one or more particular aspect of that faith.

Secularisation: a process whereby society and its institutions become free from religious control or influence.

Secularism: a belief in a non-religious view of life and society, or one that excludes, ignores or diminishes a religious understanding of life.

Secular humanism: a belief that there is no God, supernatural or spiritual force beyond that of human beings.

Spiritual: usually refers to a dimension of human life and understanding that goes beyond the physical or material, often associated with an awareness of the transcendent, self-awareness, or the power of human spirit.

Stereotypes: overgeneralisations (often erroneous and oversimplifying), often about people or groups, based on assumptions and misinformation rather than on facts. Stereotypes do not take account of the enormous diversity of the people belonging to a given group. They do not consider the current circumstances of the individual or the range of reasons why members of a group or category may differ from one another in a variety of ways. Stereotypes can lead to discriminatory behaviour, and often serve to justify prejudice.

Tolerance: it can be understood in a "weak" or "strong" sense. In its weak sense, it equates quite simply to "putting up with" – from a distance – the fact that others may live as they wish even though they may not share our values or belong to the same cultural or religious group. Understood in a stronger sense, tolerance goes beyond mere resigned acceptance that others are entitled to the same freedom that we enjoy and which has been granted to us by the powers in government. It implies that we consider that our own convictions are good and valid for ourselves and that those of others are equally good and valid in their eyes and that it is not for us to pass judgement on their conception of what constitutes a "good life".

Values: attitudes or concepts held to be of great worth or importance by an individual, group or religious tradition, usually the product of or leading to certain beliefs.

Sales agents for publications of the Council of Europe
Agents de vente des publications du Conseil de l'Europe

BELGIUM/BELGIQUE
La Librairie Européenne -
The European Bookshop
Rue de l'Orme, 1
B-1040 BRUXELLES
Tel.: +32 (0)2 231 04 35
Fax: +32 (0)2 735 08 60
E-mail: order@libeurop.be
http://www.libeurop.be

Jean De Lannoy
Avenue du Roi 202 Koningslaan
B-1190 BRUXELLES
Tel.: +32 (0)2 538 43 08
Fax: +32 (0)2 538 08 41
E-mail: jean.de.lannoy@dl-servi.com
http://www.jean-de-lannoy.be

CANADA
Renouf Publishing Co. Ltd.
1-5369 Canotek Road
OTTAWA, Ontario K1J 9J3, Canada
Tel.: +1 613 745 2665
Fax: +1 613 745 7660
Toll-Free Tel.: (866) 767-6766
E-mail: order.dept@renoufbooks.com
http://www.renoufbooks.com

**CZECH REPUBLIC/
RÉPUBLIQUE TCHÈQUE**
Suweco CZ, s.r.o.
Klecakova 347
CZ-180 21 PRAHA 9
Tel.: +420 2 424 59 204
Fax: +420 2 848 21 646
E-mail: import@suweco.cz
http://www.suweco.cz

DENMARK/DANEMARK
GAD
Vimmelskaftet 32
DK-1161 KØBENHAVN K
Tel.: +45 77 66 60 00
Fax: +45 77 66 60 01
E-mail: gad@gad.dk
http://www.gad.dk

FINLAND/FINLANDE
Akateeminen Kirjakauppa
PO Box 128
Keskuskatu 1
FIN-00100 HELSINKI
Tel.: +358 (0)9 121 4430
Fax: +358 (0)9 121 4242
E-mail: akatilaus@akateeminen.com
http://www.akateeminen.com

FRANCE
La Documentation française
(diffusion/distribution France entière)
124, rue Henri Barbusse
F-93308 AUBERVILLIERS CEDEX
Tél.: +33 (0)1 40 15 70 00
Fax: +33 (0)1 40 15 68 00
E-mail: commande@ladocumentationfrancaise.fr
http://www.ladocumentationfrancaise.fr

Librairie Kléber
1 rue des Francs Bourgeois
F-67000 STRASBOURG
Tel.: +33 (0)3 88 15 78 88
Fax: +33 (0)3 88 15 78 80
E-mail: francois.wolfermann@librairie-kleber.fr
http://www.librairie-kleber.com

**GERMANY/ALLEMAGNE
AUSTRIA/AUTRICHE**
UNO Verlag GmbH
August-Bebel-Allee 6
D-53175 BONN
Tel.: +49 (0)228 94 90 20
Fax: +49 (0)228 94 90 222
E-mail: bestellung@uno-verlag.de
http://www.uno-verlag.de

GREECE/GRÈCE
Librairie Kauffmann s.a.
Stadiou 28
GR-105 64 ATHINAI
Tel.: +30 210 32 55 321
Fax.: +30 210 32 30 320
E-mail: ord@otenet.gr
http://www.kauffmann.gr

HUNGARY/HONGRIE
Euro Info Service
Pannónia u. 58.
PF. 1039
H - 1136 BUDAPEST
Tel.: +36 1 329 2170
Fax: +36 1 349 2053
E-mail: euroinfo@euroinfo.hu
http://www.euroinfo.hu

ITALY/ITALIE
Licosa SpA
Via Duca di Calabria, 1/1
I-50125 FIRENZE
Tel.: +39 0556 483215
Fax: +39 0556 41257
E-mail: licosa@licosa.com
http://www.licosa.com

MEXICO/MEXIQUE
Mundi-Prensa México, S.A. De C.V.
Río Pánuco, 141 Delegacion Cuauhtémoc
06500 MÉXICO, D.F.
Tel.: +52 (01)55 55 33 56 58
Fax: +52 (01)55 55 14 67 99
E-mail: mundiprensa@mundiprensa.com.mx
http://www.mundiprensa.com.mx

NETHERLANDS/PAYS-BAS
Roodveldt Import BV
Nieuwe Hemweg 50
1013 CX Amsterdam
The Netherlands
Tel.: + 31 20 622 8035
Fax.: + 31 20 625 5493
Website: www.publidis.org
Email: orders@publidis.org

NORWAY/NORVÈGE
Akademika
Postboks 84 Blindern
N-0314 OSLO
Tel.: +47 2 218 8100
Fax: +47 2 218 8103
E-mail: support@akademika.no
http://www.akademika.no

POLAND/POLOGNE
Ars Polona JSC
25 Obroncow Street
PL-03-933 WARSZAWA
Tel.: +48 (0)22 509 86 00
Fax: +48 (0)22 509 86 10
E-mail: arspolona@arspolona.com.pl
http://www.arspolona.com.pl

PORTUGAL
Livraria Portugal
(Dias & Andrade, Lda.)
Rua do Carmo, 70
P-1200-094 LISBOA
Tel.: +351 21 347 42 82 / 85
Fax: +351 21 347 02 64
E-mail: info@livrariaportugal.pt
http://www.livrariaportugal.pt

**RUSSIAN FEDERATION/
FÉDÉRATION DE RUSSIE**
Ves Mir
9a, Kolpacnhyi per.
RU-101000 MOSCOW
Tel.: +7 (8)495 623 6839
Fax: +7 (8)495 625 4269
E-mail: orders@vesmirbooks.ru
http://www.vesmirbooks.ru

SPAIN/ESPAGNE
Mundi-Prensa Libros, s.a.
Castelló, 37
E-28001 MADRID
Tel.: +34 914 36 37 00
Fax: +34 915 75 39 98
E-mail: libreria@mundiprensa.es
http://www.mundiprensa.com

SWITZERLAND/SUISSE
Planetis Sàrl
16 chemin des pins
CH-1273 Arzier
Tel.: +41 22 366 51 77
Fax: +41 22 366 51 78
E-mail: info@planetis.ch

UNITED KINGDOM/ROYAUME-UNI
The Stationery Office Ltd
PO Box 29
GB-NORWICH NR3 1GN
Tel.: +44 (0)870 600 5522
Fax: +44 (0)870 600 5533
E-mail: book.enquiries@tso.co.uk
http://www.tsoshop.co.uk

**UNITED STATES and CANADA/
ÉTATS-UNIS et CANADA**
Manhattan Publishing Company
468 Albany Post Road
CROTTON-ON-HUDSON, NY 10520, USA
Tel.: +1 914 271 5194
Fax: +1 914 271 5856
E-mail: Info@manhattanpublishing.com
http://www.manhattanpublishing.com

Council of Europe Publishing/Editions du Conseil de l'Europe
F-67075 Strasbourg Cedex
Tel.: +33 (0)3 88 41 25 81 – Fax: +33 (0)3 88 41 39 10 – E-mail: publishing@coe.int – Website: http://book.coe.int